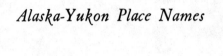

Alaska-Yukon Place Names

James W. Phillips

Alaska-Yukon Place Names

UNIVERSITY OF WASHINGTON PRESS
Seattle & London

Copyright © 1973
by the University of Washington Press
Printed in the United States of America

Library of Congress Cataloging in Publication Data

Phillips, James Wendell, 1922–
    Alaska-Yukon place names.

    Bibliography: p.
    1. Names, Geographical—Alaska. 2. Names,
Geographical—Yukon Territory. I. Title.
F902.P45   917.98'003   73–1776
ISBN 0–295–95259–8

Dedicated to the only real treasure that accrued to my grandfather from his participation in the Alaska-Yukon Gold Rush of 1898—a daughter, Goldie Nugget McLaughlin Phillips

Preface

THIS alphabetically arranged dictionary details the origins and meanings of names for cities, towns, and a representative sampling of remote native (both Eskimo and Indian) villages in the state of Alaska and the Yukon Territory. In addition, it includes the name sources of many geographical features that, in my opinion, are of historical or current news significance.

For the further edification of visitors and residents new to the Northland, this book also covers the way points along the inland and marine routes throughout Alaska, the Yukon Territory, and the pertinent coast and northern sections of British Columbia. To heighten understanding of the region, its history, and its development, many less prominent place names are included because they explain the flora and fauna (Fireweed Creek, Ptarmigan, Whale and Walrus islands), geology and topography (Gold Creek, Platinum, Silver City, Pingaluk River), and exploration and settlement (Bering Sea, Malaspina and Muir glaciers, Cook Inlet, Mount Vancouver, Sixtymile River, Hydaburg, Watson Lake).

The selection of communities is based on 1970 census reports, 1972 postal directories, and current gazetteers issued by various agencies of the governments involved in the Northland. To assure that a broad spectrum of tourist attractions was provided for readers, another major source of place/feature names has been the "where-to-go, what-to-see" pamphlets and guides published by both government and private travel agencies, tour operators, airlines, steamships, and ferries.

Several entities in a given area frequently have the same name derived from the same source, such as Juneau (city, mountain, harbor, ice field, island, lake) and Taku (arm, community, glacier, harbor, inlet, mountain, point, range). In the interest of brevity, only one entry—that of the community or, in the absence of a settlement, the major geographic feature—appears in the text on the assumption the reader will extend the generic definition appropriately. In instances where place names commence with a geographical term such as cape, lake, mount, or point, those of communities are entered in the text by such designations (Point Hope); those of geographical features are listed under their main name (Laberge, Lake).

Often the origin or evolution of a name has been explained by a variety of accounts, some of which are apocryphal. In all such cases I have given what is in my judgment the best documented, most logical explanation. Where no definition currently exists (or one has not come to my attention), the entry so states, while providing whatever information concerning the site is available.

A phonetic pronunciation guide is a part of each entry, except in the case of common or obvious words. It should be noted, however, that pronunciation occasionally varies from locale to locale and between old-timers and newcomers, particularly in the case of Anglicized names of Eskimo, Indian, and Russian origination. The pronunciations shown in this book were coordinated by individuals officially versed in regional place names and represent the most accepted general usage at the present time.

Although archives have been searched and local experts contacted, corrections and clarifications in definitions and pronunciation are inevitable (and expected). Hence, readers with information on places mentioned or omitted are invited to send documentation to the author in care of the publisher so that future editions can be revised and expanded.

Obviously, in a work of this scope and complexity, the author is indebted to a variety of research sources. Prime references included other historians and the archives of museums, libraries, and historical societies throughout the Pacific Northwest. Without the cooperation and expertise of postal and civic officials, scholars, lay experts, and sourdoughs who granted me interviews and responded to query letters, this book certainly could not have been completed.

The publications and personal assistance of Donald J. Orth, director of the Geographic Names Section, Geological Survey, U.S. Department of the Interior, and president of the American Name Society, have been invaluable. In addition, I would like to acknowledge the very special assistance provided by Phoebe Harris and her history department staff at the Seattle Public Library. Other history specialists who provided material—often their own research notes—included Roy S. Minter, vice-president, corporate communications, White Pass & Yukon (railway) Route; aviation writer Stephen E. Mills; Michael E. Dederer, vice-president of Jay Rockey Public Relations, Inc., special consultants to the State of Alaska; and Professor Charles J. Keim, College of Arts and Letters, University of Alaska.

I am appreciatively indebted to three official representatives of the State of Alaska: Lee C. Kramer, manager of the Seattle Information Office of the Department of Economic Development; and Phyllis Nottingham and Robert N. De Armond of the State Historical Library in Juneau.

The Yukon government officials who rendered special service to me were Karl L. Crosby, manager, and Marjorie Robertson, counselor, Yukon House, Vancouver, B.C., and territorial archivist Brian Spiers, Whitehorse Library—all representatives of the Yukon Department of Travel Information.

JAMES W. PHILLIPS

Seattle, Washington
12 November 1972

Introduction

PLACE names—the titles of communities and geographic features that currently appear on maps—provide a mute, but richly descriptive, account of the history of the State of Alaska and the Yukon Territory. Bestowed by native inhabitants, explorers, and adventurers, the names chronologically detail the impact of various ethnic cultures and nationalistic groups upon the vast Northland.

Native place names show the sectors initially occupied by the Eskimos, the Aleuts, and the several diverse linguistic groups and tribes of Indians that inhabited the region. Russian names and the Slavic transliteration of native names recall the invasion of tsarist fur traders into the Aleutian Islands and the coastal areas of Alaska. Intermixed with the Russian titles are a host of English and a sprinkling of Spanish names assigned by naval explorers from Britain and Mexico (New Spain). Inland the Indian names are interspersed with those affixed by traders and voyageurs of the Hudson's Bay Company and by the adventurers of various nationalities, most often Americans, who prospected for gold.

Later, waves of scientific explorers—American, British, and Canadian military men, government surveyors, and visiting scholars—covered the hinterland, mapping remote areas, confirming and consolidating earlier data, and bestowing names. Patriotic by personality and sponsorship, these men utilized the names of superiors, colleagues, and notables of their respective governments. They varied the procedure occasionally by honoring a renowned scientist of another country or by affirming a name already bestowed by one of their earlier foreign counterparts. But in the main the names they laid upon the land continued the nationalistic pattern. Hence, the place names of Alaska and the Yukon graphically explain the region's history—its exploration, its settlement, and the phases of development or use that it has undergone.

Actually, the early exploration of Alaska and the Yukon can be attributed to a series of six quests: (1) the search for the Northwest Passage, the mythical northern waterway linking the Atlantic and Pacific oceans; (2) the hunt along coastal waters for sea otter skins to capitalize on the lucrative China trade; (3) the inland efforts of Canadian fur-trading companies to secure prime pelts for European markets; (4) the competitive attempts by the colonization-minded world powers to find and claim new lands; (5) the rescue searches for British explorer Sir John Franklin, who became stranded in the Arctic Ocean with 134 crewmen; and, as always, the most comprehensive in geographic scope, (6) man's consuming penchant for gold prospecting.

Vitus Bering, a Danish-born navigator in the employ of the Imperial Russian Navy, was commissioned by Tsar Peter the Great to determine if the Asian and American continents were joined or separate. Bering made two voyages, 1728 and 1741, to determine where the northern ocean waters led and what lands they touched. On the first voyage he sailed north along the Asian coast past that continent's most northeasterly tip (East Cape) and back to his expedition's base on the Kamchatka Peninsula via what is now known as Bering Strait and Bering Sea. En route, he sighted and named one of the Diomede Islands, but failed to see the Alaska coast even though a scant fifty-five miles separates the Asian and North American mainlands.

On the second voyage both of the expedition's ships, the *Saint Peter* commanded by Bering and the *Saint Paul* captained by Alexei

Chirikov, sighted North America. Chirikov raised land on 15 July 1741 in the Alexander Archipelago, where sixteen of his crew mysteriously disappeared while attempting to gain the shore. Chirikov sailed back to Kamchatka by way of the Aleutian Islands, where he had one brief encounter with Aleuts who supplied water to his starving, scurvy-ridden crew.

Bering sighted Mount Saint Elias on 16 July 1741 and subsequently landed on Kayak Island. Fauna and flora observations by the German-born naturalist, Georg Steller, confirmed that the expedition had in fact landed on the North American continent. And thus Alaska was "officially" discovered.

The sixty-year-old Bering and nearly half of his crew died of scurvy, but the news and luxurious furs the survivors carried back to Siberia launched the Russian invasion of Alaska. Rugged, ruthless *promyshlenniki,* freebooting fur hunters, moved eastward from the Komandorskie Islands into the Aleutians. As they exterminated sea otter, fur seals, and blue foxes—and many of the Aleuts—on the westernmost islands, they moved ever closer to the mainland. Eventually organized under the control of Grigorii Ivanovich Shelikhov, the hunters founded the first permanent white settlement in Alaska at Three Saints Harbor, Kodiak Island, in 1783. In 1790 the Shelikhov Company acquired a new director of American interests, Alexander Andreevich Baranov. Nine years later the company was rechartered as the monopolistic Russian-American Company and Baranov became its general manager.

For the next twenty-eight years, Baranov autocratically ruled both the company and the land. He moved the headquarters first to Saint Paul Harbor on Kodiak Island and then to Sitka in the Alexander Archipelago. Upon retirement, he was followed as manager-governor by a series of thirteen naval officers, during whose reigns much of the coast south of the Arctic Circle was charted and named.

From Bering's discovery of Alaska in 1741 until the sale of Russian America to the United States in 1867, the Russians avidly assigned names to the land: Slavic-language personal and descriptive names, and muddled adoptions and adaptations of native titles. Today, the Russian era is commemorated by innumerable historic place names. Bering is honored, as are many of his crew including Lt. Alexei Chirikov, Lt. Sven Waxel, scientist Georg Steller, and a seaman named Shumagin, the first European to be buried in Alaska soil. Early fur hunters' namesakes include the Andreanof, Korovin, and Pribilof islands and Shelikof Strait. Russian governors and naval explorers are remembered through the names of such prominent places as Baranof Island, Etolin Island, Wrangell, Kotzebue, and Shishmaref.

In the later part of the eighteenth century, Spain attempted to solidify its claim to lands north of the Columbia River by sending Mexico-based naval explorers to Puget Sound, Vancouver Island, and Alaska. In the 1770s and 1780s Juan Francisco de la Bodega y Quadra, Salvador Fidalgo, and Alessandro Malaspina cruised, charted, and named in Southeastern Alaska as evidenced by present-day Cordova, Bucareli Bay, Malaspina Glacier, and Revillagigedo Island. However, Spain lost an attempt to enforce exclusive claims to an area centered on Nootka Sound (Vancouver Island) and passed from the regional scene in 1795.

Spain's archrival in the worldwide contest for land possession by right of exploration had also ventured north to Alaska. In 1776 England had sent the Royal Navy's Capt. James Cook, the most world renowned explorer of the era, to seek out a Pacific Ocean entrance to the supposed Northwest Passage. From March to October 1778, Captain Cook was in Alaska waters, venturing above the Arctic Circle to a point south of Point Barrow which, as further progress was blocked by ice floes, he appropriately named Icy Cape. He explored every major easterly opening, including Cook Inlet, and when its twisting upper channel forced his H.M.S. *Resolution* to turn back again, he called it Turnagain Arm. After decorating the coast with such British titles as Bristol, Darby, Edgecumbe, Fairweather, Norton, Prince William, and Prince of Wales, he sailed to the Sandwich (Hawaiian) Islands, where in February 1779 he was killed by natives.

The names of several of his crewmen (William Bligh of eventual H.M.S. *Bounty* infamy, George Vancouver, James King, Nathaniel Portlock, and George Dixon) are reminders of the early Alaska voyages of Cook and his cohorts.

Three of his crew returned to Pacific Northwest waters as captains: Vancouver, commanding a Royal Navy exploration expedition to support Cook's verdict that no Northwest Passage existed, and Port-lock and Dixon in fur trading vessels. All three extensively named sectors of the Alaska coast, particularly Vancouver, who officially charted the water passages and islands east and south of Kodiak Island. While, in the best tradition, he confirmed previously assigned Russian and Spanish names, he also assigned a myriad of typically English names that honored his home, sovereign, superiors, fellow officers, and crewmen: Berners Bay and Lynn Canal, Clarence Strait and Coronation Island, Admiralty Island and Hood Bay, Puget Cape and Whidbey Passage.

The explorations of Cook and Vancouver, their reports on the availability of animal pelts and the furs' worth in China accelerated commercial Alaska junkets by English and American adventurers, and even sparked a quick scientific expedition by France. In the main, these latter visitors had minimal name impact on the western coast of the Northland. The quest for furs and the still-active interest in a northern link—even an ocean-river-portage route—from the Pacific to Atlantic oceans was, however, beginning to make inroads into the Northland from its eastern side.

The first white man to set foot in what is now the Yukon Territory was Sir John Franklin, a Royal Navy captain, who walked across the northern reaches of the Yukon in 1825, seeking clues to a Northwest Passage. Starting from the interior of Canada, he followed the Mackenzie River down to the Arctic Ocean and then hiked west along the shoreline into Alaska. By plan, Franklin was to have rendezvoused somewhere along his westward trek with Capt. Frederick W. Beechey in the H.M.S. *Blossom,* but ice at Point Barrow forced Beechey to retrace his course and Franklin to retrace his steps.

Both left names on the Arctic coast that exist today: Beechey dubbed Points Wainwright, Franklin, and Barrow; Franklin left a host of titles including Beechey Point, Prudhoe Bay, Beaufort Sea, Herschel Island, and the British Mountains.

Franklin made a sea voyage in search of a northern water route in 1845–47. His two ships and 134 crewmen were lost and became the subject in the next decade of more than forty searches—motivated by rewards of cash and public fame for the rescuer—that did more than any single factor (up to the recent oil explorations) to map and chart the Northland's Arctic area.

In the 1830s the Hudson's Bay Company encroached upon, then leased from the Russian-American Company, a trading post site at the mouth of the Stikine River in Southeastern Alaska that gave the English access to their trading and trapping areas in northern British Columbia. In 1834 one of the company's traders, Robert Campbell, moved northward in his quest for furs and thus became the first non-native to venture into the interior of the Yukon. Son of a Scottish sheep farmer, Campbell was a tireless explorer who spent virtually all of the next twenty years in the Yukon. He discovered and named the Pelly, Stewart, and Lewes (upper Yukon) rivers; built Fort Selkirk; and in 1851 descended the unknown course of the Yukon River. When he reached its juncture with the Arctic-born Porcupine River, he serendipitously found Fort Yukon, which the Hudson's Bay Company had trespassingly established in 1847 in violation of Russian sovereignty.

The latter half of the nineteenth century witnessed many changes in the Northland. Ownership of Russian America (Alaska) was transferred on 18 October 1867 to the United States. The Yukon area became a part of Canada's Northwest Territories. Sea otter and fur seal hunting waned, but whalers discovered the mammalian wealth of the Bering Sea. Coastal communities grew and inland trading post settlements were sparsely scattered throughout the interior wilderness. Government representatives (among them Canadian surveyors George M. Dawson and William Ogilvie, and conservationist John

Muir, geologist-hydrographer William Healey Dall, and Lieutenants Henry T. Allen and Frederick Schwatka of the United States), as well as scientists of other nations, explored, mapped, charted, surveyed, and studied the resources and natural phenomena of the Northland, often with little regard for or awareness of the ill-defined boundaries that separated the United States from Canada. Their efforts contributed great knowledge and a multitude of names, which were mostly either sycophantic, honoring country, superiors, and celebrities, or else definitive titles intended to eliminate confusing duplications, scientific inaccuracies, or meaningless obscurities. Many of these "improved" names were adopted at the expense of more suitable, better-sounding native names.

The last major impact on the Northland's history and nomenclature was perhaps the most significant of all. Gold!

The existence of mineral wealth in the Northland was no secret. Baranov knew of it, and the Russians even briefly mined it on the Kenai Peninsula in the 1850s. The early Hudson's Bay Company explorers and trappers knew of it; Robert Campbell found "gold colors" at Fort Selkirk, and a clerk at Fort Yukon wrote letters describing a stream containing so much gold it could be "gathered with a spoon." The men then on the scene were fur trappers and traders only interested in the wealth afforded by prime pelts, but the news of gold spread and drew professional prospectors from the British Columbia strikes on the Fraser River and in the Cassiar Mountains, from the played-out or staked-out mother lodes of the western United States, even from the gold fields of Australia and South Africa. These men, experienced and hardened, moved slowly but methodically into every sector of the Northland—always searching, sometimes finding, continually naming.

The first big strike in the Juneau area in 1880 stepped-up the quest for pay dirt both in geographic scope and the intensity of effort and numbers. A United States gunboat demonstrated the workings of a gatling gun to a coastal band of Tlingit Indians who had forceably kept the Chilkoot Pass closed to outsiders in order to preserve their own trade monopoly with the Indians of the interior. The pass promptly opened and prospectors filtered over the natives' route to the Yukon River basin.

Gold was soon found in payload quantities and boom camps sprang into being: Fortymile in 1886, Circle City in 1893, and Dawson City in 1896. It was the latter mining camp, born of Siwash George Carmack's gold discovery on a tributary to the Klondike River, that became the mecca of the adventurous the world over. Miners and greenhorns, gamblers and merchants, whores and conmen flocked north by the tens of thousands to garner their share of the riches of the Yukon. Most were American, most were ill-equipped physically or materially for the rigors of the land, and most did not know—or care —that the Klondike was in Canada's newly formed Yukon Territory rather than Alaska.

By 1898 Dawson City boasted a population of 30,000, with another 15,000 living along the banks of nearby, gold-rich Bonanza, Eldorado, and Hunker creeks. Alaska port towns of Dyea, Skagway, Saint Michael, and Valdez boomed as outfitting and embarkation centers. The routes to the diggings—the Chilkoot and Dalton trails, White Pass, the Stikine, Fraser, and Mackenzie rivers—were clogged with humanity as an estimated 200,000 people headed north. By 1900 the Klondike boom had busted. Some of the gold-seekers headed home, a few wealthy, most broke, many broken. Some stayed on in hinterland settlements, some in marked (and unmarked) graves. Some pushed on to new strikes in Nome, Ophir, Fairbanks, Atlin, or Keno Hill.

Wherever prospectors went in Alaska and the Yukon, they applied names. The reasons behind the choice of these names are seldom recorded, but collectively they tell the tale of the men who searched the land they wandered. There are nostalgic "back home" names (Boston Dome, California River, Montana Gulch, Pennsylvania Creek, Vermont Pass) and patriotic titles (Fourth of July Creek, Canadian Creek). The miners named sites for the minerals they sought (Galena, Gold Dust Creek, Platinum, Silver City) and the women they had known (Elsa, Ester Creek, Dorothy Creek,

Sarah Gulch). The names they picked reflected their hopes (Maybe Creek, Last Chance Creek), their frustrations (Hard Luck Creek, Hoodoo Gulch, Fool Creek), their hardships (Graveyard Creek, Starvation Creek, Coldfoot), even their diet (Bean Creek, Bacon Creek, Moonshine Creek, Bourbon Creek, Whiskey Creek, Sweetcake Creek). They used the names of plants and animals and descriptive geographic terms, as well as their own surnames, to identify the geography and thereby left a vivid record of what and who was where and when.

In the twentieth century, railroad and highway builders, the fishing, lumbering, and oil industries, the military, tourism, and transportation have joined forces to create a new chapter in the chronicle of the Northland. This progress is reflected in additions to and adaptations of the place names of Alaska and the Yukon. However, the old and the new names, the original versions and the evolutionary alterations, still detail the history of the Northland. The names bestowed by the native population of Eskimos on the Arctic and western coasts, Aleuts in the southwest, the several tribes of Athabascan Indians in the interior, and the Tlingit, Haida, and Tsimshian Indian tribes in the southeastern sectors live on, augmented by the informative titles affixed by explorers, miners, scientists, and settlers.

Pronunciation Guide

Accented syllables appear in capital letters, unaccented syllables in lower-case letters (Island = EYE-luhnd).

AY	GRAY, BAY, SALE
A	CAT, RAN
AH	TOP
AW	BOUGHT, SAW
AIR	CARE, FAIR
EE	SEE, TREAT
E	BET, SAID
ER	CURVE, SMIRK
EYE	SIGHT, FLY
I	BIT
IR	PIERCE
OH	SEW
OW	OUT, ROUND, ALLOW
OO	BOOT, SUIT, ROOF
OO̲	FOOT, SHOULD, BUSH
OI	BOY, POINT
OR	DOOR, BOARD
YOO	CUE, MENU
UH	CUP, AGAIN, TOUGH
CH	CHIN
G	GUN
J	JUNK
S	SALARY, CELERY

Abbreviations

AFB	United States Air Force Base
AFS	United States Air Force Station
H.M.S.	His Majesty's Ship
IRN	Imperial Russian Navy
RCMP	Royal Canadian Mounted Police
RN	(British) Royal Navy
S.S.	Steamship
USA	United States Army
USAF	United States Air Force
USCG	United States Coast Guard
USC&GS	United States Coast & Geodetic Survey
USCS	United States Coast Survey
USGS	United States Geological Survey
USN	United States Navy
USRCS	United States Revenue Cutter Service
U.S.S.	United States Ship
USSR	Union of Soviet Socialist Republics

Alaska-Yukon Place Names

GEOGRAPHIC LOCATION GUIDE

Each place name listing in the text includes an identifying abbreviation that will enable readers to determine quickly the site's geographic location.

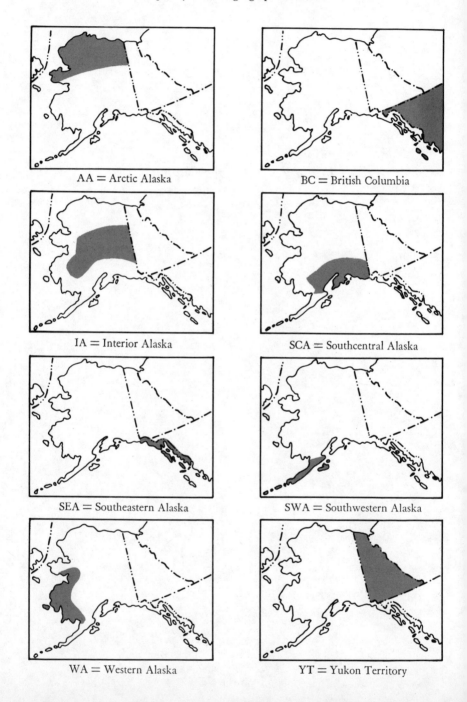

AA = Arctic Alaska

BC = British Columbia

IA = Interior Alaska

SCA = Southcentral Alaska

SEA = Southeastern Alaska

SWA = Southwestern Alaska

WA = Western Alaska

YT = Yukon Territory

A

Adak Island, AY-dak (SWA). Site of a strategic USN facility and one of the Andreanof Islands, the island purportedly derives its name from the Aleut word *adaq,* meaning "father."

\ **Admiralty Island** (SEA). Named in 1794 by Capt. George Vancouver to honor the Board of Admiralty of Great Britain, which supervised the RN and authorized his own circumnavigation of the world, 1790–95, in search of the mythical Northwest Passage. A midshipman on Capt. James Cook's voyage to Alaska in the late 1770s, Vancouver in 1793–94 extensively explored and charted the Pacific coast of North America from Lower California to the Alaska Peninsula. His ships, *Discovery* and *Chatham,* covered some 65,000 miles and left an estimated 300 British place names along the route. [*See* Lynn Canal; Vancouver, Mount.]

Adolphus, Point (SEA). North tip of Chichagof Island that extends into Icy Strait (opposite the Gustavus Point entrance to Glacier Bay) was named in 1794 by Capt. George Vancouver, RN, to honor Adolphus Frederick, one of the fifteen children of King George III of England. [*See* Frederick, Port; Gustavus.]

Afognak Island, uh-FAWG-nak (SWA). The island's name is a native word of unknown meaning adopted by the Russians in the mid-1700s and logged by Capt. George Vancouver in 1794 as "what the Russians call Fogniak." Early in the 1800s, a settle-

3

ment of retired employees of the Russian-American Company was established on the island. In 1964 the village was destroyed by an earthquake and resultant tidal wave, and the residents removed to a new community, Port Lions, built for them on adjacent Kodiak Island. [*See* Port Lions.]

Agassiz Glacier, AG-uh-see (SEA). Glacier in the Saint Elias Mountains and a point north of Petersburg honor Louis Agassiz, Swiss-born naturalist who taught at Harvard University, 1848–73.

Agattu Island, AG-uh-TOO (SWA). A corruption of the Aleut name Agataku, of unknown meaning. Agattu is one of the Near Islands.

Aiktak Island, EYEK-tuhk (SWA). An Aleut word affixed by the Russians to this island in the Krenitzin group and probably derived from *aikhak,* meaning "to travel." [*See* Rootok Islands.]

Aishihik, AYSH-ee-ak (YT). Indian word meaning "high place." The road to the lake and abandoned village, now used only as a summer fishing camp, passes Otter Falls, which are depicted on Canadian five-dollar bills.

Akiak, AK-kee-ak (WA). Name stems from an Eskimo term meaning "crossing over," as the natives moved across the delta from this Kuskokwim River site to the Yukon River each winter.

Akun Island, AK-koon (SWA). Island name was derived by Lt. Peter Kuzmich Krenitzin, IRN, in 1768 from the Aleut word *hakun,* meaning "that over there." [*See* Krenitzin Islands.]

Akutan Island, AK-kuh-tan (SWA). The name of this Krenitzin group island is purportedly an adaptation of the Aleut word *hakuta,* meaning "I make a mistake."

Alakanuk, uh-LAK-uh-nuk (WA). Community derives its name from its location at the east end of Alakanuk Pass, a waterway between channels at the mouth of the Yukon River. This Eskimo name for the delta maze of watercourses aptly means "wrong way."

Alaska, uh-LAS-kuh. Commonly accepted to mean "great land," the name is derived from the Aleut term variously spelled Alashka, Alaesksu, and Alyeska that was used by those natives to differentiate the mainland from their islands. When in 1867 the United States purchased the region internationally known as Russian America, a new title was obviously needed. Among the names suggested were Aleutia, Aliaska, Oonalaska, Sitka, Yukon, and Walrussia, a humorous contraction of walrus and Russia. Although credit for the suggestion of the final choice has been alternately attributed to Secretary of State William H. Seward, Massachusetts Senator Charles Sumner, or Gen. Henry W. Halleck of the Pacific Division, USA, the selection was, in essence, a popular extension of the already established name of the Alaska Peninsula (prominently so marked on long-existing maps) to the whole region. Alaska, purchased for a price of $7,200,000, comprises 586,400 square miles, which are encompassed by 33,000 miles of coastline. It contains 10 rivers over 300 miles long, 3 million lakes larger than 20 acres, more than half of the world's glaciers, and 19 mountains higher than 14,000 feet, including Mount McKinley, 20,320 feet, the tallest peak in North America. And as an added oddity, Alaska boasts the northernmost (Point Barrow), westernmost (Amatignak Island), and easternmost (Semisopochnoi Island) points in the United States. Alaska was changed from a possession to a territory in 1912 and given statehood in 1959. [*See* Juneau.]

Alaska Chief Falls (SEA). Name taken from nearby Alaska Chief Claim staked by Joseph Juneau and Richard Harris, which, in turn, was named for their canoe. [*See* Juneau.]

Alaska Highway. *See* Alcan Highway.

Alaska Range (IA). This mountain range stretches 650 miles across the center of Alaska from the east end of the Alaska Peninsula to the Yukon Territory border. Midpoint in the range is Mount McKinley National Park. Highest peaks in the range are Mount McKinley, 20,320; Mount Foraker, 17,395; and Mount Hunter, 14,573. [*See* McKinley, Mount.]

Alatna, uh-LAT-nuh (IA). Name of this Eskimo village is a corruption of the original Indian name for the Allakaket River. [*See* Allakaket.]

Alava, Point, uh-LAH-vuh (SEA). Southern tip of Revillagigedo Island was named by Capt. George Vancouver, RN, in 1793 to honor José Manuel de Alava, who succeeded Capt. Juan Francisco de la Bodega y Quadra as Spanish commissioner at the Nootka Convention. [*See* Boca de Quadra.]

Alcan Highway. This name is a shortened form of Alaska-Canada Military Highway, the original name of the present Alaska Highway that stretches 1,523 miles from Dawson Creek, B.C., through 630 miles of the Yukon Territory to Fairbanks, Alaska. Construction of the World War II land route to Alaska was begun on 2 March 1942 by the U.S. Army Engineers, and a traversable road was completed nine months later.

Aleknagik, uh-LEK-nuh-gik (WA). Village takes its name from that of the adjacent lake, which derives from an Eskimo descriptive term literally meaning "dotted with [pine] tree-covered islands."

Aleutian Islands, uh-LOO-shun (SWA). Named for the Aleuts, an Eskimoid people native to the partially submerged extension of the Alaska Peninsula that arcs 1,200 miles southwesterly from the mainland. The treeless, semivolcanic archipelago consists of five major groups of islands—Fox, Four Mountains, Andreanof, Rat, and Near—that separate the Pacific Ocean from the Bering Sea. Center of the breeding grounds for sea otter, the chain was discovered by the Russians in 1741, victimized by fur and whale hunters in the 1800s, and invaded by the Japanese in World War II. The Japanese bombed Dutch Harbor on Unalaska Island on 3 June 1942 and simultaneously landed troops on various westerly islands in the chain, primarily Attu and Kiska. In August 1943, exactly 493 days after invasion, combined U.S. ground, sea, and air forces regained complete control of the Aleutians.

Alexander Archipelago (SEA). Name assigned by the USC&GS in 1867 to honor Alexander II, tsar of Russia at the time Russian

America was sold to the United States. The group consists of approximately 11,000 islands—the tops of submerged mountains separated by deep channels—that vary in size from 2,231 square miles to rock tips barely jutting above the water surface at high tide. The six largest islands are Prince of Wales and Chichagof (each bigger than Delaware), Admiralty, Baranof, Revillagigedo, and Kupreanof (each larger than Rhode Island). Baranof Island served as the seat of Alaska government for Russia from 1804 until 1867 and for the United States until 1906. [See Sitka.]

Alexander Glacier (SEA). A mountain and a glacier in the Saint Elias range were named in 1905 by the USC&GS presumably for Beno Alexander, one of the porters on the duke of the Abruzzi's ascent of Mount Saint Elias in 1897. [See Quintino Sella Glacier.]

Alexander, Lake (SEA). Lake on Admiralty Island was named in 1907 for Annie M. Alexander, founder of the University of California Alexander Alaska Expedition.

Alexander, Point (SEA). Discovered by Master James Johnstone of the H.M.S. *Chatham* and named by Capt. George Vancouver, RN, in 1793 for English architect Daniel Asher Alexander. [See Johnstone Point.]

Alitak, AL-i-tak (SWA). Originally known by the Russian-affixed name of Akhoik derived from the native name, Oohaiack, this Kodiak Island village was renamed Alitak during World War I.

Allakaket, AL-luh-KAK-et (IA). A Koyukuk Indian name meaning "mouth of the Alatna" River. In 1906, Episcopal Archdeacon Hudson Stuck established a mission near the confluence of the Alatna and Koyukuk rivers, where two native villages already existed. Allakaket, on the south bank, was for Indians and Alatna, on the opposite bank, was for Eskimos. [See Alatna.]

Allen Glacier (SCA). A glacier in the Chugach Mountains and a river in the Brooks Range honor Lt. Henry Tureman Allen, USA, who covered 1,500 miles in the interior of Alaska from 20 March to 28 August 1885. An aide to the Alaska commandant, Gen. Nelson A. Miles, Allen started his journey at the Copper River and after traveling on the Tanana, Yukon, and Koyukuk rivers, ended at Saint Michael. He named many geographical features along the route and his maps remained standard works for a decade. [*See* Glennallen.]

Alverstone, Mount (SEA). The 14,500-foot peak straddling the Alaska-Canada border in the Saint Elias Mountains was named in 1908 to honor England's Lord Chief Justice Richard Everard Webster, Viscount Alverstone. He was one of "six impartial jurists of repute" who comprised the Alaska Boundary Tribunal of 1903 charged with resolving the Alaska-British Columbia border controversy. The United States' representatives appointed by President Theodore Roosevelt were former Senator George Turner of Washington State, Senator Henry Cabot Lodge of Massachusetts, and Secretary of War Elihu Root. In addition to Lord Alverstone, the British members named by the crown were Sir Louis Jetté, lieutenant governor of Quebec, and John D. Armour, judge of the Supreme Court of Canada, who was replaced after his death in 1903 by Sir Allen Bristol Aylesworth, noted Toronto attorney. Lord Alverstone voted with the American block, and Canada lost its hopes for a more westerly boundary and seaports along the Panhandle. Boundary-straddling peaks in the Saint Elias range bear the names of all seven men who served on the international boundary commission.

Alyeska, Mount, AL-ee-ES-kuh (SCA). The 3,939-foot mountain in the Chugach Mountains was named in 1959 by the U.S. Forest Service for the Alyeska Ski Area on its slopes. The name is one of the various spellings of the state's name. [*See* Alaska.]

Amak Island, uh-MAK (SWA). Name derived by the Russians from the Aleut word *amaq,* meaning "blood."

Amaknak Island, uh-MAK-nak (SWA). This island in Unalaska Bay was named for an old burial cave on its southwest shore which derived its name from the Aleut word *amaiknaq,* meaning "place of impurity."

Amatignak Island, am-uh-TIG-nak (SWA). Bearing an Aleut

name meaning "wood chips," this island in the Delarof group is the southernmost island of the Aleutian chain. It is also the westernmost point in the United States, as it lies 20 miles on the Alaska-mainland side of the 180th meridian, which divides the Western and Eastern hemispheres. [*See* Barrow; Semisopochnoi Island.]

Ambler (AA). Founded in the late 1950s, this community derives its name from a tributary of the Kobuk River. The name honors Dr. James M. Ambler, USN, who died of starvation in the Lena River delta after the U.S.S. *Jeannette,* under command of Lt. Comdr. George Washington De Long, was trapped in the Arctic ice pack in 1881. [*See* De Long Mountains.]

Amchitka Island, am-CHIT-kuh (SWA). An Aleut name of unverified meaning. One of the Rat Islands, it was the site of a controversial Atomic Energy Commission underground nuclear test blast in November 1971.

Amlia Island, am-LEE-uh (SWA). The name for this island in the Andreanof group is a Russian adaptation of its original Aleut name, Amlak, of unknown meaning.

Amukta Island, uh-MUHK-tuh (SWA). The most westerly of the Islands of the Four Mountains has an Aleut name of unknown meaning. Adjacent passage from the Pacific Ocean to the Bering Sea was called Seventy-second Pass by American whalers because of its proximity to longitude 172° west.

Anaktuvuk Pass, an-nuhk-TOO-vuhk (AA). Pass and Eskimo village names derive from the river of the same name. The river's title stems from the native word *anaq* pertaining to "place where dung is found."

Anchorage (SCA). Situated on a broad peninsula between Knik and Turnagain arms of Cook Inlet, Alaska's largest city was founded on the banks of Ship Creek in 1913 as construction headquarters for the proposed Seward-to-Fairbanks Alaska Railroad. It was first known as Ship Creek, then Woodrow, and finally in 1914 received its present name derived from the boat anchorage at the mouth of Ship Creek. Ocean vessels, unable to reach the then-existent town of Knik at the head of Knik Arm, transferred their cargo to lighters offshore from the stream, and the last deepwater site thus became known as Knik Anchorage. The government town was to be named Woodrow for President Wilson, but on 2 August 1914 the townspeople voted for their choice among several possibilities. The results were: Anchorage, 101; Matanuska, 54; Ship Creek, 48; Winalaska, 18; Terminal, 16; Gateway, 10; and Homestead, 9.

Anchor Point (SCA). Name of the community on the Kenai Peninsula was adopted from that of a nearby point where Capt. James Cook, RN, lost an anchor in 1778.

Anderson (IA). Arthur Anderson, who platted his homestead at this site into residential lots, named the town after himself.

Andreanof Islands, AN-dree-an-nawf (SWA). Translation of Andreianovski Ostrova, the Russian name for this group of islands first explored in 1761 by fur merchant Andreian Tolstyk in his ship, *Andreian and Natalia,* named for himself and his wife. [*See* Aleutian Islands.]

Andronica Island, an-DRAW-ni-kuh (SWA). The name of this member of the Shumagin Islands is adapted from the Russian, Ostrov Apostola Andronika, meaning "Island of Apostle Andrew."

Angoon, an-GOON (SEA). This town on Admiralty Island bears a Tlingit name initially recorded as Augoon, of unknown meaning. [*See* Killisnoo Harbor.]

Aniak, AN-ee-yak (WA). Founded as a trading post around 1910, the community takes its name from the adjacent river, whose name was recorded by Russian navy explorers as Anniak, of unknown meaning.

Annette, uh-NET (SEA). Community owes its name to its location on Annette Island, in the Alexander Archipelago, which was named by William Healey Dall, USC&GS, in 1879 in honor of his wife, Annette Whitney Dall. [*See* Dall Island.]

Anvik, AN-vik (WA). Community name and that of the Yukon River tributary come from the Koyukon dialect (of the Athabascan linguistic group) name for a centuries-old native village at the site known prosaically as "place of the louse eggs"—a blight the inhabitants combated with daily sweat baths and urine rinses.

Anvil Range (YT). Name derives from the anvillike appearance of a peak in this silver-rich group.

Archdeacons Tower (IA). The 19,650-foot peak in Mount Mc-Kinley National Park honors the Episcopal archdeacon of the Yukon, Hudson Stuck, who was a member of the first party officially to scale Mount McKinley on 7 June 1913. The tower is at the head of Harper Glacier, named for Walter Harper, another member of the party that climbed McKinley's 20,320-foot South Peak. [*See* McKinley, Mount.]

Arctic Ocean, ARK-tik. The ocean north of the Arctic Circle gets its name from the Greek word *arktos,* meaning "bear," a derivative of which—*arktikos*—ancient astrologers applied to the constellation, Ursa Major, that circumscribes the polar region. The deepest part of the 5,541,000-square-mile ocean is 17,850 feet, in the Chukchi Sea north of Bering Strait.

Arctic Slope. The Arctic Mountain System—consisting of the De Long, Baird, Schwatka, Endicott, Philip Smith, and Davidson mountains and the Brooks Range in Alaska, and the British and Richardson mountains of the Yukon Territory—rise to 10,000 feet and separate the interior plain from the region to the north. This latter area declining northward toward the Arctic Ocean is known as the Arctic Slope. It is permafrost (always frozen beneath the surface) land nearly devoid of trees, and the majority of its rivers flow to the Arctic Ocean. [*See* North Slope.]

Arctic Village (AA). Village on the East Fork Chandalar River bears a name descriptive of its location. In speaking, Alaskans generally pronounce the word "arctic" without the first "c"—"AHR-tik."

Arey Island, AIR-EE (AA). Because the original name, Barter Island, bestowed in 1826 by Sir John Franklin, RN, was applied in local usage to a larger island to the east, the island's name was changed in 1907 by Ernest de Koven Leffingwell of the Anglo-American Polar Expedition. The new name honored a local prospector, Ned Arey, who had assisted the scientist in exploration. [*See* Barter Island.]

Armour, Mount (SEA). The peak straddling the Alaska-Canada border in the Saint Elias Mountains was named jointly in 1923 by the U.S. Board on Geographic Names and the Canadian Permanent Committee on Geographical Names to honor Canadian Supreme Court Judge John D. Armour, an original member of the Alaska Boundary Tribunal of 1903. [*See* Alverstone, Mount.]

Asses Ears (WA). Twin 200-foot-high peaks that rise above the Seward Peninsula's Black Butte were given this descriptive name by Lt. Otto von Kotzebue, IRN, on 11 August 1816. [*See* Black Butte.]

Atka Island, AT-kuh (SWA). Largest of the Andreanof group, the island bears a native name of unknown definition and a 4,852-foot volcano with a name derived from the Russian word *korova,* meaning "cow." "Atka" possibly stems from an Aleut term variously recorded as *atchu* and *atghka.* The volcano's name, Korovin, is an adoption of the surname of a trader who sailed southwestern Alaska waters in the 1760s. [*See* Korovin Island.]

Atlin, AT-luhn (BC). Community was founded as a mining camp in 1898 with the discovery of gold on the east shore of Atlin Lake by Fritz Miller and Kenny McLaren. The name is an adaptation of the Indian name *aht-lah,* meaning "stormy water." [*See* Discovery; Miller House.]

Attu Island, AT-too (SWA). Westernmost of the Aleutian Islands' Near group, the island was first visited in 1742 by Lt. Alexei Ilich Chirikov, IRN, whose name is commemorated by a point at its eastern tip. The name is an Aleut word of unknown meaning. [*See* Chirikof Island.]

Augusta, Mount (SEA). The 14,070-foot mountain that straddles the Alaska-Canada boundary in the Saint Elias Mountains was named by Israel Cook Russell, USGS, for his wife, J. Augusta Olmstead Russell. [*See* Russell, Mount.]

Augustine Island (SCA). The site of 4,025-foot high Augustine volcano, the island was named Saint Augustine by Capt. James Cook, RN, in 1778. The Russian name for the island was Ostrov Chernoburoi, a descriptive "black-brown."

Auke Bay, AWK (SEA). Town name is that of the Auk subdivision of Tlingits, who primarily lived in the Juneau-Berners Bay area. The term derives from *aku,* meaning "little lake." One of the few native names in the locality not discarded by early miners, it is often repeated in local geography: it appears in the title of a cape, creek, lake, and mountain; in Auk-an or "lake town"; Auke nu, meaning "Auk fort" in Tlingit; and Auk Bay on the Kenai Peninsula. [*See* Mendenhall Glacier.]

Avatanak Island, uh-VAT-nak (SWA). The name for this member of the Krenitzin Islands was an Aleut term adopted by the Russians and phonetically spelled and misspelled in a variety of ways by a successive host of navigators and cartographers (as was frequently the case in the early era of exploration) until the original word and its definition were lost. [*See* Rootok Island.]

Aylesworth, Mount (SEA). The peak straddling the Alaska-Canada border in the Saint Elias Mountains was named by the USC&GS in 1908 to honor Sir Allen Bristol Aylesworth, a noted Toronto attorney, who was appointed to the Alaska Boundary Tribunal of 1903 upon the death of Canadian jurist John D. Armour. [*See* Alverstone, Mount.]

B

Babbage River (YT). Arctic Slope river was named in 1826 by Sir John Franklin, RN, for a contemporary scientist, Charles Babbage, one of the founders of the British Astronomical Society. [*See* Herschel Island.]

Babine River, BA-been (BC). A French term meaning "extended lip" was applied by Hudson's Bay Company voyageurs to the Indians in the area because the women wore bone or wooden labrets in their lower lips.

Bagley Icefield (SCA). Named in 1951 by the USGS to honor one of its topographers, Col. James Warren Bagley (1881–1947).

Bainbridge Island (SCA). Island, passage, point, and glacier in the Kenai Peninsula area were named by Capt. George Vancouver, RN, in 1794 to honor British astronomer John Bainbridge. However, Bainbridge Peak in Southeastern Alaska (as well as Bainbridge Island in Puget Sound, Washington State) was named by American naval officers to honor Commodore William Bainbridge, USN, hero of the war with Tripoli and the War of 1812.

Baird Mountains (AA). Range northeast of Kotzebue Sound and an inlet east of Nelson Island honor naturalist Spencer F. Baird (1823–87), secretary of the Smithsonian Institution, first U.S. fisheries commissioner, and North American bird expert.

Baker Island (SEA). The island in the western portion of the

Prince of Wales Archipelago was named in 1879 by William Healey Dall, USC&GS, to honor government cartographer Marcus Baker. After surveying the Alaskan coast from Dixon Entrance on the south to the Point Barrow area in the Arctic, Baker assisted Dall in the compilation of the *1883 Coast Pilot.* He subsequently authored the first *Geographic Dictionary of Alaska,* published by the U.S. Geological Survey in 1902. [*See* Point Baker.]

Baldwin Peninsula (AA). The 75-mile-long peninsula that juts into Kotzebue Sound was named in 1933 by Carl J. Lomen, a commercial reindeer rancher and processor, for New York financier Leonard D. Baldwin, who had invested $1.5 million in the Lomen Reindeer Company.

Baranof Island, BAIR-uh-nawf (SEA). Name of this Alexander Archipelago island honors a shopkeeper's son and once-bankrupt Siberian merchant, Alexander Andreevich Baranov, 1746–1819, the first governor of Alaska. He joined the Shelikhov Company as manager at Three Saints Harbor in 1790; founded Saint Paul Harbor (Kodiak) as the main trading headquarters in Alaska in 1792; and in 1804 established Novoarkhangelsk (New Archangel) on the west coast of Baranof Island as the trading and administrative headquarters of Russian America. As general manager of the monopolistic Russian-American Company, which succeeded the Shelikhov Company in 1799, Baranov served as governor of the Russian colonies in North America until his retirement in 1818. [*See* Sitka.]

Barren Islands (SCA). So named by Capt. James Cook, RN, in 1778 for "their very naked appearance."

Barrow, BAIR-oh (AA). The town, the world's largest Eskimo community, adopted its name from nearby Point Barrow to replace the native name Utkiakvik, meaning "high ground for viewing," with one easier for nonnatives to pronounce. The point was named by Capt. Frederick W. Beechey of the H.M.S. *Blossom* in 1826 to honor Sir John Barrow, secretary of the British Admiralty, who actively promoted Arctic explorations. Point Barrow is the northernmost point in the United States. [*See* Amatignak Island; Semisopochnoi Island.]

Barter Island (AA). Initially, Sir John Franklin, RN, mistakenly believed the island to be part of the mainland and called it Point Manning. He gave the name Barter to a small island to the west. However, local usage prevailed: originally called Katoavik by the Eskimos, the large island, a long-established native trading site, became Barter Island, and the smaller island was subsequently renamed Arey Island. [*See* Kaktovik.]

Bearpaw City (IA). Former mining camp is a typical example of the descriptive and imaginative names assigned to Alaska's topography by prospectors, trappers, and explorers. The land of the bear—the giant brown, the black, the grizzly, the rare blue glacier, the Kodiak, and the Arctic polar—has more than 150 geographic features with variations of the faunal name, such as Bear Blanket Slough, Bearhole Creek, Bearnose Hill, Bearpaw City, Bearskin Gulch, Beartrack Island, Beartrap Bay, and 57 Bear Creeks.

Beaufort Sea, BOH-fert. Part of the Arctic Ocean abutting Alaska and the Yukon Territory was named in 1826 by Sir John Franklin, RN, for a fellow navy officer, Sir Francis Beaufort, British Admiralty hydrographer. [*See* Prudhoe Bay.]

Beaver (IA). Eskimo-Indian village on the Yukon River just south of the Arctic Circle was established in the early 1900s as a river landing. With the short-lived Chandalar gold strike around 1911, it was known briefly as Beaver City. It is one of more than 80 places and geographic features—lakes, mountains, creeks, rivers, dams, bays—in Alaska to bear some variation of this faunal name.

Beaver Creek (YT). Site of the Canadian Customs Immigration Station at Milepost 1202 on the Alaska Highway, the community adopted its name from the pre-1900 descriptive faunal title of the adjacent stream. The actual Alaska-Canada border is to the west at Milepost 1221.8. [*See* Port Alcan.]

Beaver Mountains (IA). Purportedly a faunal name given by early prospectors.

Becharof Lake, buh-SHAIR-awf (SWA). This lake and a peak and stream on the Alaska Peninsula were named by William Healey Dall in 1868 to honor an IRN navigator based at Kodiak Island in the 1780s.

Bede, Point, BAY-dee (SCA). Point on northwestern tip of the Kenai Peninsula derives its name from Capt. James Cook, RN, who charted the locality on 26 May 1778, the eve of Saint Bede's Day.

Beechey Point, BEECH-ee (AA). The most westerly promontory visible from the Prudhoe Bay area was named 17 August 1826 by Sir John Franklin for Capt. Frederick W. Beechey, RN, who had been slated to rendezvous with Franklin on the coast of the Beaufort Sea during his search for the Northwest Passage. The ice pack at Point Barrow (named by Beechey for Sir John Barrow, secretary of the British Admiralty) forced his ship to turn west again, and the failure to meet forced Franklin to retrace his steps back to the Mackenzie River. [*See* British Mountains; Franklin, Point.]

Behm Canal, BEEM (SEA). Water passage separating Revillagigedo Island in the Alexander Archipelago from the mainland was named in 1793 by Capt. George Vancouver, RN, to honor Maj. Magnus Carl von Behm, a German who, while serving as Russian commandant of Kamchatka, assisted the Cook expedition in 1779.

Belcher, Point (AA). Named by Capt. Frederick W. Beechey, RN, in 1826 for Lt. Edward Belcher, assistant surveyor on the H.M.S. *Blossom.* [*See* Franklin, Point.]

Belkofski, bel-KAWF-skee (SWA). Village has a faunal name derived from the Russian word *belka,* meaning squirrel.

Beluga, buh-LOO-guh (SCA). Community, river, and lake on north side of Cook Inlet bear the common name for a species of white whale derived from the Russian word *beluga.* [*See* Whale Island.]

Bendeleben Mountains, BEN-duh-lay-ben (WA). Name derived from that of the highest peak in the range, which was named in 1866 for Baron Otto von Bendeleben of the Western Union Telegraph Expedition, who had explored the interior of the Seward Peninsula the previous year.

Bennett, Lake (BC). Lake at the end of the Skagway–White Pass trail of '98 was named in 1883 by explorer-writer Lt. Frederick Schwatka, USA, for James Gordon Bennett, patron of American geographical expeditions and news-making editor of the New York *Herald,* who sponsored reporter Henry M. Stanley's African search for Dr. David Livingstone. [*See* Lindeman, Lake; White Pass.]

Bering Sea, BAIR-ing. Name of the northern part of the Pacific Ocean and the strait that connects it to the Arctic Ocean honors Capt. Comdr. Vitus Bering, a Dane in the employ of the Imperial Russian Navy, who is credited with the official discovery of Alaska. Tsar Peter the Great sent Bering on a voyage in 1728 to determine if the Asian and American continents were joined or separate, and on that voyage Saint Lawrence Island was sighted and named. In 1741 Bering in the *Saint Peter* and Lt. Alexei Chirikov in the *Saint Paul* began a major voyage of discovery during which Bering sighted Mount Saint Elias on the Alaskan mainland and touched shore on Kayak Island. Chirikov, separated from the expedition commander by storms, raised land in the Alexander Archipelago. Both ships sighted the Aleutian Islands on the return voyage. Chirikov successfully returned to home port, but Bering was shipwrecked and died of scurvy on an island (later named for him) near Kamchatka, Russia. The strait was named for its discoverer by Capt. James Cook, RN, in 1778. The sea, previously called Sea of Kamchatka, was renamed in his honor by Capt. Vasilii M. Golovnin, IRN, in 1822. [*See* Saint Elias Mountains.]

Berners Bay (SEA). The bay on the east shore of Lynn Canal was assigned his mother's maiden name by a homesick and ailing Capt. George Vancouver, RN. Other nostalgic names in the vicinity assigned by Vancouver toward the end of his sojourn in Alaska waters in 1794 include Point Bridget for his mother's given name, Point Saint Mary for her birthplace, Point Mary after his sister, Port Houghton and Holkam Bay for towns in his native Norfolk, and Point Couverden in honor of the home of his forebears (van Couverdens), the Dutch city of Couvoorden. He even took possession of the region for King George III under the name of New Norfolk, a geographic designation that has passed from Alaska maps. [*See* Lynn Canal; Vancouver, Mount.]

Bethel, BETH-uhl (WA). An old Eskimo village called Mum-trekhlogamute, meaning "smokehouse people," became the site of a Moravian mission in 1885 and was given the Hebrew name for "house of God" by missionaries William H. Weinland and John H. Kilbuck. The name is found in the Biblical passage: ". . . God said unto Jacob, Arise, and go up to Bethel, and dwell there . . ." (Gen. 35:1). [*See* Kilbuck Mountains.]

Bettles Field, BET-uhlz (IA). Also known locally as Evansville, the community resulted from the construction of an airfield in 1945 and drew its population and name from nearby Bettles. That village had developed in 1899 around a trading post founded by Gordon C. Bettles, pioneer merchant and printer.

Big Delta (IA). Established as McCarty Telegraph Station by the USA Signal Corps in 1904, the community changed its name to conform with that of an area post office operating in the town from 1925 to 1959. The name Big Delta came into being to pinpoint the community's location at the juncture of the Tanana and Delta rivers and to differentiate it from Delta Telegraph Station on nearby Little Delta River. [*See* Delta Junction.]

Birchwood (SCA). This suburb of Anchorage has an arbitrarily selected residential development name of one of the three main species of trees—spruce, birch, and aspen—native to the area.

Bitzshtini Mountains, BITCH-uhs-TEE-nee (WA). Adaptation of a Tanana Indian term relating to "caribou."

Blackburn, Mount (IA). Located in the Wrangell Mountains, the 16,390-foot mountain is Alaska's fifth highest and was named in 1855 by Lt. Henry Tureman Allen, USA, for Kentucky Senator Joseph Clay Stiles Blackburn. [*See* Allen Glacier.]

Black Butte (WA). This 2,073-foot-high mountain on the Seward Peninsula was so named in 1950 by the USGS because its underbase of exposed marble and promontory covered by dark lichen gave it a stark, black-on-white appearance. Among the more than 140 geographic features in Alaska to include the adjective "black" in their names are Black Sand Creek, Blackface Point, Black Dog Creek, Black Duck Bay, Blackbird Island, Black Bear Lake, Black Chief Creek, Black Cap Mountain, Black Crook Creek. [*See* Asses Ears.]

Bligh Island, BLEYE (SCA). Island in Prince William Sound was explored by Master Joseph Whidbey, RN, of the Vancouver expedition in 1794 and named for Capt. William Bligh, RN. A fellow officer of Vancouver's on Captain Cook's third voyage in 1779, Bligh was commander of the 1787–89 scientific voyage to Tahiti that turned into the infamous H.M.S. *Bounty* mutiny. [*See* Cook Inlet.]

Bobrof Island, BOB-rawf (SWA). The name of this island and its volcano in the Andreanof group in the Aleutian chain derives from the islet's original Russian title, Ostrov Bobrovoi, meaning "beaver island." The early Russians mistakenly applied their word *bobr,* or beaver, to the sea otter they hunted. [*See* Otter Island.]

Boca de Quadra, BOH-cuh day KWAH-druh (SEA). The "estuary of Quadra" entering Revillagigedo Channel at the Keta River honors Spanish Capt. Juan Francisco de la Bodega y Quadra. The name was assigned by Lt. Jacinto Caamaño in 1792 in recognition of his superior and was confirmed the following year by Capt. George Vancouver, RN, who was Quadra's English counterpart in the Nootka Sound meetings to negotiate British-Spanish territorial claims on the northwest coast of America. [*See* Revillagigedo Island.]

Bolshoi Islands, BOHL-shoi (SWA). Small islands off the coast of Atka Island take their name from the largest of the group, originally called Ostrov Bolshoi or "large island" in Russian.

Bompas, Mount, BAHM-puhs (YT). Peak in the Saint Elias Mountains honors Rev. William Bompas, first bishop of the Church of England's Diocese of Yukon, who spent from 1865 to 1905 as a missionary in the Northland. [*See* Carcross.]

Bona, Mount, BOH-nuh (IA). Located in the Wrangell Mountains, Alaska's fourth highest mountain (16,500 feet) was named by Luigi Amedeo Giuseppe Maria Ferdinando Francesco, the duke of the Abruzzi, Italian naval officer and explorer, after his yacht *Bona,* meaning "good." [*See* Lucania, Mount; Quintino Sella Glacier.]

Bonanza Creek (YT). Stream on which George Washington Carmack staked his discovery claim, on 17 August 1896, that sparked the Klondike Gold Rush was originally known as Rabbit Creek. Five days after the claim was filed, a miners' meeting gave the gold-laden stream the Spanish name "Bonanza," literally meaning "smooth sea," hence good luck or richness in ore. Other rich streams in the immediate locale were named Eldorado, the Spanish name for a legendary treasure city in the Americas sought by early conquistadors; Hunker, after its discoverer, Andrew Hunker; and Gold Bottom, where Robert Henderson made the initial—if personally unrewarding—gold find in the Klondike River basin. [*See* Carmacks; Gold Bottom Creek; Hunker Creek.]

Boundary (IA). The first stop in Alaska on the road west from Dawson, Y.T., this settlement derives its name from its proximity (3 miles) to the border.

Bradfield Canal (SEA). Named in 1793 by Capt. George Vancouver following its exploration by Master James Johnstone of the H.M.S. *Chatham*. [*See* Johnstone Point.]

Brady Glacier (SEA). Name honors Rev. John Green Brady, governor of Alaska from 1897 to 1906.

Brevig Mission, BRE-vig (AA). Community at the site of the Teller Reindeer Station, founded on the Seward Peninsula in 1892 by Presbyterian missionary Sheldon Jackson, honors T. L. Brevig. Brevig was assistant to Jackson and a teacher at the station from 1894 to 1898. After a two-year sojourn stateside, Brevig returned as a Lutheran minister to the station, where he founded an orphanage. Following establishment of the nearby town of Teller around 1900, the station became known as Teller Mission and adopted its present name in 1963 when a post office was established incorporating Brevig's name. [*See* Teller.]

Bristol Bay, BRIS-tuhl (WA). Named in 1778 by Capt. James Cook, RN, to honor Adm. Augustus John Hervey, 3rd earl of Bristol and a lord of the British Admiralty, 1771–75. [*See* Chatham Strait.]

British Columbia. The westernmost province of Canada has been known, as a whole or in part, by a variety of titles. It was part of a vast area dubbed "New Albion" by Sir Francis Drake in 1579. In 1792–94 Capt. George Vancouver, RN, subdivided the region into three sectors: he called Vancouver Island "Quadra and Vancouver's Island"; the south coast section, including Oregon and Washington, "New Georgia"; and the north coast section, "New Hanover." In the early 1800s the region was considered part of the Oregon Country, while Hudson's Bay Company explorers attempted to apply the names "New Caledonia" to the central portion and "Stikeen Territory" to the northern portion. Most maps and exploration accounts, however, vaguely lumped the land mass north of Spanish California and south of Russian America under the general heading "Columbia," the name of the region's greatest river. The present name was personally and purposefully coined as an identifying geographic and nationalistic title by Queen Victoria when she created the mainland crown colony in 1858. The Stikeen (from the Stikine River) Territory and

Vancouver Island became part of British Columbia in 1863 and 1866, respectively, and the colony became a province of the Dominion of Canada in 1871. Third largest of the country's ten provinces (and more than one-third larger than the Yukon Territory), British Columbia encompasses 359,279 square miles. Victoria is its capital and Vancouver is its largest city.

British Mountains (YT). Range straddling the Arctic sector of the Alaska-Yukon border was named in 1825 by British explorer Capt. Sir John Franklin, RN, the first white man to set foot upon Yukon soil. Franklin led three expeditions in search of an Arctic Atlantic-Pacific water route, in 1819–22, 1825–27, and 1845–47. On the last, Franklin, 134 men, and 2 ships were lost and became the subject of more than 40 land and sea searches, 1847–59, during which much of Arctic Alaska and Canada was explored and charted. [See Prudhoe Bay.]

Brooks Range (AA). Name is among many throughout Alaska that honor chief Alaskan geologist Alfred Hulse Brooks, USGS, who spent from 1898 to 1924 in exploration and mineral examination of the wilderness areas of what was then the Territory of Alaska.

Browne Tower (IA). The 14,600-foot promontory in Mount McKinley National Park was named by Episcopal Archdeacon Hudson Stuck in 1913 to honor Belmore Browne, who was a member of a party that failed to reach the mountain's summit the previous year. [See McKinley, Mount.]

Bucareli Bay, boo-kuh-REL-lee (SEA). Named on his first voyage to Alaska in 1775 by Capt. Juan Francisco de la Bodega y Quadra to honor Mexico's 46th viceroy, Antonio María Bucareli y Ursúa Henestrosa Lasso de la Vega Villacis y Cordova, who authorized the voyage. [See Orca Bay; Suemez Island.]

Buckland (AA). Community on the Seward Peninsula takes its title from that of the adjacent river named in 1826 by Capt. Frederick W. Beechey, RN, to honor a professor of geology at Oxford University.

Buldir Island, BUHL-der (SWA). This member of the Rat Island group was first shown as Ostrov Buldir by a Russian naval cartographer in 1791. The name has two possible origins. First, it may be a later-day attempt to commemorate Stefan Buldirev, a cooper aboard Capt. Comdr. Vitus Bering's *Saint Peter* who died of scurvy near an island in the area which Bering sighted and named Saint Stefan on 28 October 1741. Or the name could be descriptive of the island's shape, from the Russian word *buldyr'*, meaning "hut."

Burns Lake (BC). The geographical center of British Columbia, this town is named for telegraph route explorer Michael Byrnes, who conducted a survey in the area around 1866. [*See* Telegraph Creek.]

Burwash Landing, BER-wahsh (YT). Community on shore of Kluane Lake was established in 1903 by Eugene and Louis Jacquot and named for Maj. Lockwood Burwash, a government mine recorder.

Butte, BYOOT (SCA). Community centered on the Glenn Highway takes its name from nearby Bodenburg Butte, the isolated, 888-foot-high hump dominating the Matanuska Valley.

C

Caamano Point, kuh-MAY-noh (SEA). Spanish explorer Lt. Jacinto Caamaño gave his name to the southern tip of Cleveland Peninsula in 1792. [*See* Revillagigedo Island.]

Cache Creek, KASH (IA). The term *cache,* meaning "hiding place," came to the Northland with French-Canadian fur trappers and refers to the practice of storing supplies and furs in a safe, but not necessarily secret, place, often in a tree or stilt-legged house where edibles were secure from prowling animals.

Camden Bay (AA). Named by Sir John Franklin in 1826 to honor prominent British peer John Jeffreys, the 1st marquess of Camden.

Campbell Mountains (YT). Mountain range and the highway crossing it honor Hudson's Bay Company explorer-trader Robert Campbell, the first white man to venture into the interior of the Yukon Territory. The Scottish-born Campbell spent 20 years, 1834–53, in the wilderness of western Canada exploring the Stikine, Pelly, Upper Yukon, and Stewart river areas and in 1848 built the company's key Yukon trading post, Fort Selkirk, at the confluence of the Lewes and Pelly rivers. [*See* Simpson Range.]

Campion Air Force Station, KAMP-ee-uhn (IA). Situated north of Galena, this USAF installation was named in honor of 1st Lt. Alan Campion, USAF, whose F-94 crashed near the site in 1950.

Canada. The name is derived from the Iroquois Indian term *kanata,* meaning "a collection of dwellings." It was first recorded in 1535 by French explorer Jacques Cartier, discoverer of the St. Lawrence River, who presumably believed the name of his Indian guides' "town" also applied to the area in which they lived. In land area, Canada is the second largest country in the world, with 3,851,809 square miles. Of its ten provinces and two territories, British Columbia, containing 359,279 square miles, ranks fourth in size behind the Northwest Territories, Quebec, and Ontario; while the Yukon Territory, with 205,346 square miles, is eighth.

Candle (AA). Mining community in the center of the Candle Creek placer gold district received its name from a scrubby bush growing in the area that the Eskimos—and early miners—burned to illuminate their dwellings.

Canol Road, KAN-awl (YT). The name of the service road to Norman Wells in the Northwest Territories is a short form of Canadian Oil Pipeline Highway.

Cantwell (IA). Community name is an adoption from nearby Cantwell Creek, a headwater tributary to the Nenana River which was briefly called "Cantwell River" in honor of Lt. John C. Cantwell, USRCS.

Cape Lisburne Air Force Station, LIZ-bern (AA). Situated north of Kotzebue on Cape Lisburne, this USAF installation takes its name from that promontory, which was discovered and named by Capt. James Cook, RN, in 1778.

Cape Newenham Air Force Station, NOO-uhn-ham (WA). The USAF installation bears the title of the south Bering Sea point on which it is situated. The cape was initially named by an officer in the exploration force of Capt. James Cook, RN, in 1778. The landfall was one of the sites where Captain Cook's men took possession of the region in the name of the king of England by planting a bottle containing a slip of paper on which were written the names of the H.M.S. *Discovery* and H.M.S. *Resolution* and the date of discovery.

Cape Pole (SEA). The community name is a tie-in to nearby Cape Pole on the southwest coast of Kosciusko Island. The point was named in 1793 by Capt. George Vancouver for a Royal Navy fellow officer, Capt. Morice Pole. The island was named a century later (via pun, association, or coincidence?) by William Healey Dall, USC&GS, to honor a Polish-born hero of the American Revolutionary War. [*See* Kosciusko Island.]

Cape Romanzof Air Force Station, roh-MAN-zawf (WA). The USAF installation bears the title of the Bering Sea point on which it is situated. The cape was initially named by Lt. Gleb Shishmarev, IRN, to honor Count Nikolai Rumiantsev, who built the 180-ton brig *Rurik* to search for the Northwest Passage. [*See* Kotzebue; Romanzof Mountains.]

Cape Yakataga, YAK-uh-TAG-uh (SEA). Name of community is a Tlingit Indian word meaning "canoe road," because two reefs form a narrow boat passage to the bay on the eastern side of the cape.

Carcross, KAHR-krahs (YT). A contraction of the original descriptive name, Caribou Crossing, suggested by a Church of England missionary, Bishop William Bompas, in 1905 to avoid confusion with similarly titled sites. [*See* Bompas, Mount.]

Carlisle Island (SWA). Named in 1894 by the USC&GS to honor the then secretary of the treasury, John G. Carlisle, this island belongs to the Islands of the Four Mountains group.

Carmacks (YT). Named for ex-Californian George Washington Carmack who, with his Indian brothers-in-law Tagish Charlie and Skookum Jim, made the gold strike on Rabbit Creek (renamed Bonanza Creek by prospectors because of its richness in gold) on 17 August 1896. While Carmack's strike triggered the Klondike Gold Rush, he was originally touted to this area by Nova Scotian prospector Robert Henderson, who had struck color on nearby Gold Bottom Creek earlier in 1896. Though Henderson missed out on both fame and rich pay dirt, he was eventually credited as codiscoverer of the Klondike Strike by the Canadian government and awarded a monthly pension of $200. [*See* Bonanza Creek; Dawson; Gold Bottom Creek.]

Caro, KAIR-oh (IA). Ghost town on the Chandalar River was named for Caro Kingsland Clum, daughter of the Fairbanks postmaster, John P. Clum, who helped secure a post office for the short-lived mining camp in 1907.

Cassiar Mountains, KAS-ee-ahr (BC). Mountains, river, and mining district all derive their names from the Indian word *kaska,* meaning "creek."

Caton Island, KAT-uhn (SWA). A name often repeated in the Shumagin-Sanak islands area is of unverified origin. Possibly it is a transplant of the name Caton Shoal, part of a dangerous reef near Unga Island which was reported to authorities in 1880 by a Mr. Caton and apparently named for him by the USC&GS. [*See* Sanak Islands.]

Central (IA). Village in the Circle Mining District derives its name from Central House, a roadhouse on the trail to Circle.

Chalkyitsik, chawl-KIT-sik (AA). Name of this settlement in the Yukon Flats area is an Indian term meaning "to fish with a hook at creek mouth," and hence it is known by non-Indians as Fishhook Village.

Chamisso Island, chah-MIS-oh (AA). Island and waterway south of Baldwin Peninsula were named in 1816 by Lt. Otto von Kotzebue, IRN, to honor Adelbert von Chamisso. A refugee from the French Revolution and subsequently an officer in the Prussian army, Chamisso was a botanist aboard the *Rurik* during its scientific voyage around the world in 1815-18. [*See* Kotzebue.]

Champagne (YT). A former Northwest Mounted Police post and a way-stop on the famed Dalton Trail, the community was purportedly named by its founder, Jack Dalton, in 1902 as he opened a case of French champagne. [*See* Dalton Post.]

Chandalar River, CHAN-duh-lahr (IA). Tributary to the Yukon River is said to derive its name from the French spoken phrase, *gens de large,* which early French trappers of the Hudson's Bay Company used to refer to the nomadic Indians living along the river.

Chandler River (AA). Lakes and stream tributary to the Colville River were named to honor William E. Chandler, secretary of the navy from 1882 to 1885, at the time the big lake was discovered by Lt. George M. Stoney, USN.

Chatanika, chat-uh-NEE-kuh (IA). The village takes its Tanana Indian name from the adjacent Chatanika River (meaning unknown), formed by three creeks—Faith, Hope, and Charity—named by prospectors. [*See* Cleary Creek.]

Chatham Strait, CHAT-uhm (SEA). Waterway in the Alexander Archipelago extending from Coronation Island to Lynn Canal was named by Capt. George Vancouver, RN, to honor John Pitt, 2nd earl of Chatham, who was first lord of the Admiralty, 1788-94, during Vancouver's voyage. One of Vancouver's ships, the H.M.S. *Chatham,* also bore the name of the earl, who was the elder brother of Prime Minister William Pitt. [*See* Admiralty Island.]

Cheechako Gulch, chee-CHAW-koh (IA). Name applied to this ravine is an Alaska-Yukon miners' expression for a tenderfoot or greenhorn. The word comes from the multilanguage Chinook Jargon, the lingua franca of the Pacific Northwest Indians and white traders and explorers: Chinook *t'shi,* meaning "new," plus Nootka *chako,* meaning "to come." [*See* Sourdough Gulch.]

Chena River, CHEE-nuh (IA). An Athabascan Indian name combining *chee,* definition unknown, with *na,* a suffix meaning "river."

Chenan Lakes, CHEE-nan (SCA). A series of three connected lakes, known as First, Second, and Third, located on the Edgerton Highway to Chitina bears an Indian name meaning "thank you," in recognition of the fact that the lakes were well stocked with grayling.

Chernabura Island, CHERN-uh-ber-uh (SWA). The name for this Shumagin group island derives from the descriptive Russian term, *chernoburyi,* meaning "black-brown." [*See* Augustine Island.]

Chetwynd (BC). Name honors Ralph L. T. Chetwynd, former minister of railways for British Columbia.

Chevak, CHEE-vak (WA). Eskimo village in the Yukon-Kuskokwim delta has a native name stemming from a term meaning "connecting slough."

Chichagof Island, CHI-chuh-gawf (SEA). This island in the Alexander Archipelago is one of more than a dozen coastal sites that honor Adm. Vasilii Yakov Chichagov, IRN, who explored the Arctic in the mid-1760s.

Chickaloon, CHIK-uh-loon (SCA). Settlement name is an Americanization of the Indian term *chic cloon,* meaning unknown, applied to a river flowing into Turnagain Arm.

Chicken (IA). Town's name is derived from the nearby creek where miners found gold nuggets the size of chicken feed (cracked corn). Generally, the names of many geographical features in Alaska containing the term "chicken" either by itself or in combination with other words are of faunal origin, as early prospectors mistakenly referred to the ptarmigan or grouse as chickens. [*See* Ptarmigan.]

Chigmit Mountains (SCA). Name of range along the northwest shore of Cook Inlet is derived from its original Indian-German form, Tschigmit Gebirge. "Gebirge" is German for "mountain range," but the Indian basis for the Germanized "Tschigmit" is unknown. The name was assigned in 1850 by Dr. Constantin Grewingk, German scientific writer and authority on volcanoes, for whom Grewingk Glacier on the Kenai Peninsula is named.

Chignik, CHIG-nik (SWA). Three communities—Chignik, Chignik Lagoon, and Chignik Lake—derive their names from Chignik Bay which, in turn, bears a native name recorded by the Russians. The meaning is unknown, but the first syllable is similar to that of the Chigmit (from "Tschigmit," a Germanized Indian term) Mountains farther up the Alaska Peninsula.

Chilkat Pass, CHIL-kat (SEA). The pass through the Coast Mountains over which ran the Dalton Trail derives its name from the Chilkat tribe of the Tlingit Indians who lived along the western arm of Lynn Canal. [*See* Chilkoot Pass; White Pass.]

Chilkoot Pass, CHIL-koot (SEA). The pass through the Coast Mountains over which ran the gold rush trail from Dyea to Lake Lindeman derives its name from the Chilkoot tribe of the Tlingit Indians. Initially residents of the east arm of Lynn Canal, they historically used—and jealously guarded—the pass as their exclusive trade route to the Tagish Indians of the interior. Gold seekers arriving by the thousands at Skagway and Dyea flocked to this short, but rigorous, entry to the headwaters of the Yukon River. Unimagined hardships—freezing cold, drenching rain, avalanches, and rugged slopes—forced thousands to turn back, crippled or killed many hundreds, and left the hardier and more determined to lockstep over the pass to face more hardships and slim prospects of finding the riches they sought. [*See* Dyea; White Pass.]

Chirikof Island, CHIR-uh-kawf (SWA). Named by Capt. George Vancouver, RN, in 1794 to honor Lt. Alexei Ilich Chirikov, IRN, who commanded the *Saint Paul,* the second vessel of the Bering expedition of 1741.

Chisana River, chi-SAN-uh (IA). Settlement, glacier, mountain, and pass in the Nutzotin and Wrangell mountains area all derive their names from the Tanana-Athabascan Indian term *chistna,* meaning "red river," used by local natives to describe a major tributary to the Tanana River. [*See* Chisna River.]

Chisna River, CHIS-naw (IA). Short river southeast of Paxson bears as its name a dialectical term meaning "red river," from the Tanana Indian word *chis,* "red," and the Athabascan generic suffix *na,* meaning "river." A former mining settlement variously known as Chisna and Dempsey was once located on the stream's banks. [*See* Chisana River.]

Chistochina, CHIS-toh-CHEE-nuh (IA). Name is derived from an Indian term meaning "marmot creek."

Chitina, CHIT-naw (SCA). The name of this community on the Copper River is an Indian equivalent for "copper river."

Cholmondeley Sound, CHAWM-lee (SEA). Bay on the east shore of Prince of Wales Island was named by Capt. George Vancouver, RN, in 1793 for the earl of Cholmondeley. In speaking, Alaskans have followed the British habit of shortening the peer's tongue-twisting name to a simple "CHAWM-lee."

Choris Peninsula, CHOR-uhs (AA). This southernmost extension of Baldwin Peninsula was named in 1816 by Lt. Otto von Kotzebue, IRN, to honor a member of his scientific exploration expedition, Ludovik Choris. [*See* Kotzebue.]

Chugach Mountains, CHOO-gach (SWA). Range, National Forest, and island are several features bearing an Eskimo tribal name. The range encompasses Chugach State Park, created by the 1970 state legislature.

Chuginadak Island, choo-GIN-uh-dak (SWA). The name for this member of the Islands of the Four Mountains is derived from the Aleut word *chugi,* meaning "to roast."

Chukchi Sea. CHOOK-chee. The name for this part of the Arctic Ocean north of Bering Strait is an Americanization of Chukotskoe More, the Russian name for the sea abutting the Chukot Peninsula of northeastern Siberia.

Churchill, Mount (SEA). This 15,638-foot mountain in the Saint Elias range honors Great Britain's prime minister during World War II, Winston Churchill. [*See* McKinley, Mount.]

Circle (IA). The town was founded in 1893 as the result of a gold strike on nearby Birch Creek by two half-breed prospectors grubstaked by prospector-trader Leroy Napoleon (Jack) McQuesten, who built a trading post at the site. Initially called Circle City because it was erroneously believed to be situated on the Arctic Circle, it was touted as the "largest log town in the world" in 1896 and boasted a population of 1,200, a music hall, 2 theaters, 8 dance halls, 28 saloons, and a library. The news of the Klondike strike at Dawson left Circle a virtual ghost town by the spring of 1897. [*See* McQuesten.]

Clam Gulch (SCA). Descriptive faunal name for a settlement situated on a tidal ravine of the same name on the west coast of the Kenai Peninsula.

Clarence Strait (SEA). Waterway in the Alexander Archipelago extending from Dixon Entrance to Sumner Strait was named by Capt. George Vancouver, RN, in 1793 for George III's son, Prince William Henry, the duke of Clarence, who became William IV of England. [*See* Prince of Wales Island; Prince William Sound.]

Clark, Lake (SCA). Named in 1891 by reporter A. B. Schanz of the *Frank Leslie Illustrated Newspaper* expedition for John W. Clark, chief of the Nushagak Trading Post, who discovered the lake. [*See* Port Alsworth; Tanalian River.]

Clarks Point (WA). This community is named for its location on Clarks Point in Nushagak Bay. The point was named in 1890 by the U.S. Bureau of Fisheries presumably in honor of Professor Samuel F. Clark of Williams College. However, local tradition contends the name honors John W. Clark, a long-time manager of the Nushagak station of the Alaska Commercial Company, who died in 1897. [*See* Clark, Lake.]

Clear (IA). Established during the World War I era as a railroad station named Clear Site.

Cleary Creek (IA). This tributary of the Chatanika River was one of several streams in the Fairbanks area in which Felix Pedro discovered the gold that led to the development of the "Golden Heart of Alaska." The creek, a summit on the Stease Highway, and a former mining town—all northeast of Fairbanks—were named for Frank J. Cleary, one of the early prospectors in the area. [*See* Pedro Creek.]

Cleveland Peninsula (SEA). Named in 1886 by the USC&GS to honor President Grover Cleveland.

Clinton Creek (YT). This supportive community for an asbestos mine derives its title from the nearby stream of the same name. The town, overlooking Fortymile River, was first established in 1968 and is not a revitalized gold mining camp or fur trading post.

Clover Pass (SEA). This Ketchikan suburb adopted its name from Clover Passage, a waterway named by the USC&GS in 1886 for Lt. Comdr. Richardson Clover, USN. [*See* Point Baker.]

Cohoe, KOH-hoh (SCA). This Kenai Peninsula community is named for the coho, a species of salmon native to the area.

Cold Bay (SWA). The community name was derived from that of the adjacent bay, which is a translation of the Russian Zaliv Morozovskii. Located at the extreme tip of the Alaska Peninsula, the town is also the site of the Cold Bay AFS, previously known as Fort Randall and Thornbrough Air Base.

Coldfoot (AA). This turn-of-the-century boom town was named by prospectors as an indication of their general physical condition in the Arctic climate. In 1912 the townspeople forsook Coldfoot for pay dirt on Nolan and Wiseman creeks, site of new camps named after prospectors who staked placer claims. [*See* Wiseman.]

Coleman Peak (SEA). Name assigned by the American Geographical Society in 1947 honors Canadian geology professor A. P. Coleman, who explored the Glacier Bay National Monument area in 1913.

College (IA). The Fairbanks suburb is so named because it was established in 1915 as the site for the Alaska Agricultural College and School of Mines—now the University of Alaska, the northernmost university in North America.

Columbia Glacier (SEA). This glacier in Glacier Bay National Monument was named in 1899 by the Harriman expedition for New York City's Columbia University. [*See* Glacier Bay; Harriman Glacier.]

Colville River, KAWL-vil (AA). The chief river of the Arctic Slope was named in 1837 by Peter Warren Dease and Thomas Simpson to honor Andrew Colvile, London governor of the Hudson's Bay Company, 1852–56, and brother-in-law of Thomas Douglas, 5th earl of Selkirk, who was the controlling stockholder in the Hudson's Bay Company prior to its amalgamation with the North West Company in 1821. [*See* Fort Selkirk; Harrison Bay.]

Contact Creek (BC). So named because USA engineers constructing the Alcan Highway from north and south met at the creek in October 1942. It is located three-tenths of a mile south of the first of several points where the Alaska Highway crosses the British Columbia–Yukon Territory border between Mileposts 588.4 and 627.

Controller Bay (SCA). An adaptation of the original name, Comptroller's Bay, assigned by Capt. James Cook, RN, in 1778 to honor Maurice Suckling, comptroller of the Royal Navy, whose name graces the bay's southern point. [*See* Suckling, Cape.]

Cook Inlet (SCA). Name honors British explorer Capt. James

Cook, RN, who on his third voyage to the Pacific discovered the Sandwich (Hawaiian) Islands and charted much of the northwest coast of America. Cook was in Alaskan waters from March to October 1778 and voyaged as far north as Icy Cape, where the ice pack blocked his search for a northern water route from the Pacific to the Atlantic. Cook was killed by natives in February 1779 while wintering in Hawaii pending return to Alaska. When the rest of his expedition reached England, Cook's patron, John Montagu, 4th earl of Sandwich and the first lord of the Admiralty, honored the explorer by attaching the name Cook's River to the waterway between the mainland and the Kenai Peninsula, which Cook had charted but left unnamed. In Alaska with Cook in the H.M.S. *Resolution* and H.M.S. *Discovery* were, in addition to Lt. William Bligh of subsequent *Bounty* mutiny infamy, Midshipman George Vancouver, Master's Mate Nathaniel Portlock, and George Dixon, armorer, who returned as captains to explore Alaska and leave their names along its coast. [*See* Turnagain Arm.]

Cooper Landing (SCA). The name for this Kenai Peninsula village derives from the fact that it was the boat landing on Kenai Lake nearest to Cooper Lake. The lake is presumably named after Joe Cooper, who mined in the Juneau area in the early 1880s prior to establishing mining operations on the Kenai Peninsula in 1883.

Copper Center (IA). Successive roles as a trading post in 1896, mining camp in 1898, USA Signal Corps telegraph station in 1901, and a key way point on the Valdez–Fairbanks Trail resulted in Copper Center's becoming the first "town" in Interior Alaska and the locale's major supply center. That function and its location at the juncture of the Copper and Klutina rivers gave birth to its name.

Copper River (IA). An important trade route from the coast to the mineral-rich interior, Copper River now bears a translation of its original descriptive Indian name.

Cordova, kor-DOH-vuh (SCA). The town was founded on Prince William Sound's Orca Bay in 1906 as the western terminus of the Copper River and Northwestern Railroad, which was constructed for the transportation of copper ore from the Kennecott Mine in the Wrangell Mountains to the seacoast for shipment from Alaska. Michael J. Heney of the railroad selected the title Cordova from Puerto Cordova, the original name for Orca Bay assigned by Spanish explorer Lt. Salvador Fidalgo in 1790. [*See* Orca Bay.]

Coronation Island (SEA). Sighted and named by Capt. George Vancouver, RN, on 22 September 1793, the thirty-third anniversary of the coronation of George III.

Council (WA). This ghost town was founded and named by a party of San Francisco gold seekers who struck pay dirt on Ophir and Melsing creeks and on 25 April 1898 organized the Council City Mining District. Once a roaring Seward Peninsula boom town, the community now serves as a summer cabin area for berry pickers and fishermen.

Coxe Glacier (SCA). Named by the USGS to honor the English scholar, Rev. William Coxe, whose search of Russian royal archives in 1780 resulted in a book, *Account of Russian Discoveries between Asia and America.*

Craig (SEA). Initially called Fish Egg after the nearby island, this community was then named Craig Millar after a local cannery owner and received its abbreviated form with the establishment of a post office in 1912.

Crazy Mountains (IA). Name in local usage in the 1890s; reason lost.

Crillon Glacier, KRIL-luhn (SEA). Mountain, inlet, lake, and river have names adopted from the glacier in Glacier Bay National Monument which was designated by the French explorer, Capt. Jean François de Galaup, comte de la Pérouse, in July 1786 to honor his countryman, Louis Balbis de Berton de Crillon, a general under Henri III and Henri IV and hero of the battle of

Lepanto [Návpaktos, Greece] against the Turks in 1571. [*See* La Perouse Glacier; Lituya Bay.]

Cripple (IA). Namesake of the famous Cripple Creek in Colorado, this gold-mining town enjoyed two surges of activity, 1913–18 and 1935–37.

Crooked Creek (IA). Community adopted its name from the adjacent stream, which was dubbed descriptively by early prospectors.

Cross Sound (SEA). Named by Capt. James Cook, RN, as it was discovered on Holy-Cross Day, 3 May 1778.

Curry (SCA). Originally a camp known as Dead Horse, this town underwent a name change with the establishment of an Alaska Railroad station at the site in 1922. The assigned name honored California Congressman Charles F. Curry.

D

Dall Island, DAWL (SEA). This Alexander Archipelago island is one of several features that honor scientist-writer William Healey Dall. One of Alaska's most prolific place-namers, he extensively explored Alaska from 1865 to 1899. He first came to the Northland with the Western Union Telegraph Expedition in 1865 and became director of its scientific corps in 1867. He returned stateside in 1868 and wrote a well-received book, *Alaska and Its Resources.* In 1871 he joined the USCS as acting assistant and stayed with the service—whose name was changed to USC&GS in 1878—until 1884, when he resigned to accept a post as a paleontologist and curator at the U.S. National Museum (now the Smithsonian Institution) in the employ of the USGS. He returned north on a gold and coal survey in 1895 and with the Harriman Alaska Expedition in 1899. During his years with the USCS-USC&GS he traveled the length of the Aleutian chain, north to Point Barrow, and edited the 1879 and 1883 editions of the *Coast Pilot*. [*See* Baker Island.]

Dalton Post, DAWL-tuhn (YT). This abandoned way point was built by an American, Jack Dalton, along the famed Dalton Trail of 1898, a toll path from Pyramid Harbor on Lynn Canal to Fort Selkirk on the Yukon River. [*See* Champagne; Chilkat Pass.]

Dan Creek (SCA). Former mining camp and stream on which it was located were named for prospector Dan Kain, who staked a claim there in 1911.

Davidson Mountains (AA). Name honors English-born geographer and astronomer George Davidson, 1825–1911, who joined the USC&GS in 1845 and was chief of the Pacific Coast region from 1868 to 1895 when he became a professor at the University of California. For fifty years Davidson made extensive studies of the coast and is noted for his marine charts, geographic publications, and the names he implanted along his route from Alaska to California.

Dawson (YT). Situated at the confluence of the Yukon and Klondike rivers, this town honors George M. Dawson, Canadian government geologist and Yukon explorer. The townsite was filed on and named in 1896 by trading-post operator Joseph Ladue while other early arrivers were staking the first claims on nearby Bonanza Creek. Originally called Dawson City, the community boasted a population in excess of 30,000 in 1898 and was the capital of the territory until 1953. [*See* Dawson Creek; Ladue River; Whitehorse.]

Dawson Creek (BC). The southern terminus—Mile 0—of the Alaska Highway is named in honor of George M. Dawson, a government geologist who extensively explored and surveyed the Canadian northland, 1873–1901. While making a railroad survey in 1879, the diminutive hunchback, who became director of the

Geological Survey of Canada, named a tributary of the Pouce Coupe ("cut-off thumb") River as Dawson's Brook, and the eventual city adopted a variation of the name. [*See* Dawson.]

Dease River, DEES (BC). Name honors Peter Warren Dease, Hudson's Bay Company factor who accompanied the Franklin Arctic expedition of 1825–27 and who subsequently headed, with Thomas Simpson, the company's Arctic expedition of 1837–39. Dease Inlet, a bay southeast of Point Barrow, was named on 2 August 1837 by Simpson for his "worthy colleague," Dease. [*See* Franklin Mountains; Harrison Bay.]

Deering (AA). A gold-mining supply center on the south shore of Kotzebue Sound was named for the schooner *Abbie M. Deering,* which plied the waters when the community was established at the turn of the century.

Delarof Islands, DEL-uh-rawf (SWA). This group of nine islands west of the Andreanof group in the Aleutian chain was named to honor Greek-born Eustrate Ivanovich Delarov, director of the Russian-American Company, 1784–91. [*See* Amatignak Island.]

De Long Mountains (AA). Name honors George Washington De Long, American naval officer and Arctic explorer who, with one-third of his crew, died of starvation in 1881 after their ship, the *Jeannette,* was crushed by the ice pack. The expedition was financially backed by James Gordon Bennett of the New York *Herald.* [*See* Bennett, Lake.]

Delta Junction (IA). Name derives from this town's location on the north bank of the Delta River at the junction of the Alaska and Richardson highways. Founded in 1919 as a work camp during construction of the Richardson Highway (from Valdez to Fairbanks), which opened in 1920, it was initially called Buffalo Center because it was at the center of the Alaska Bison Range, a government reserve for buffalo shipped north from the States.

Demarcation Point (AA). So named by Sir John Franklin, RN, in 1826 because it marked the boundary between Russian and British territory on the north coast of America.

Dempster Highway (YT). Named in honor of RCMP Inspector W. J. D. Dempster.

Denali Pass, duh-NAH-lee (IA). The highway from Paxson to Mount McKinley National Park, an 18,000-foot-level pass between the Churchill Peaks of Mount McKinley, and a former mining camp east of Mount McKinley National Park all bear the peak's Tanana Indian name, Denali, said to mean "home of the sun" or "the high one." [*See* Foraker, Mount.]

Destruction Bay (YT). Legend contends the name originated during the gold rush era because of the number of boats storm-wrecked at this point on Kluane Lake's shoreline. The Kluane Historical Society reports the name and the community came into being in the early 1940s during construction of the Alcan (Alaska) Highway. The name resulted from a windstorm's destruction of a USA tent camp, the aftermath of a young lieutenant's order to cut down all the trees at the site.

Dezadeash Lake, dez-DEE-ash (YT). Name is an Indian word describing a native fishing method unique to the locale, whereby pieces of white birch bark, shiny side up, were weighted on the lake's bottom to attract trout within reach of waiting spearmen.

Dillingham, DIL-ling-HAM (WA). Named in 1904 for U.S. Senator William P. Dillingham of Vermont, who conducted a legislative subcommittee tour of Alaska in 1903.

Dime Landing (WA). This community on the Koyuk River at the north end of Norton Bay adopted its name from the adjacent Dime Creek. The stream was so named by early prospectors because each pan produced "about a dime's worth of gold."

Diomede Islands, DEYE-oh-meed (AA). Name of the islands derives from Saint Diomede, on whose day—16 August—the larger of the two islands was purportedly discovered by Vitus Bering, IRN, in 1725. Russian Big Diomede and American Little Diomede are separated by the U.S.–USSR boundary, the international date line, and 2 miles of water. Little Diomede boasts an Eskimo village, and Big Diomede is the site of a Russian weather station. [*See* Little Diomede.]

Discovery (BC). Ghost town east of Atlin settled by Kenny McLaren in 1898. The 4-mile length of nearby Spruce Creek produced 25 million dollars in gold. [*See* Atlin.]

Dixon Entrance (SEA). The name of the boundary strait between Canadian and Alaskan waters honors Capt. George Dixon of the *Queen Charlotte* who, with former Cook voyage shipmate Capt. Nathaniel Portlock in the *King George,* extensively explored the coastal area in 1786–87 while engaged in otter-pelt trading for the King George's Sound Company. [*See* Portlock; Queen Charlotte Islands.]

Dolgoi Island, DOHL-goi (SWA). Name for this member of the Pavlof Islands comes from the Russian word *dolgii,* meaning "long."

Donjek River (YT). Purportedly an Anglicized version of the Indian term *armjeck,* meaning "pea vine."

Dot Lake (IA). Village takes its name from adjacent Dot Lake, possibly so named for its small size.

Douglas (SEA). A suburb of Juneau and once the site of the rich Treadwell Gold Mine that extended under Gastineau Channel, this residential community takes its name from Douglas Island, on which it is situated. The island was named in 1794 by Capt. George Vancouver, RN, for Dr. John Douglas, the bishop of Salisbury, who previously had edited the journal of Vancouver's former commander, Capt. James Cook. In 1778 Captain Cook had honored his Scottish friend, who was then the canon of Windsor, by naming a cape on the Alaska Peninsula after him. [*See* Douglas, Cape; Marmion Island.]

Douglas, Cape (AA). One of two capes named Douglas in Alaska. The northernmost is on the Seward Peninsula northwest of Nome and was named by Capt. Frederick W. Beechey, RN, of the H.M.S. *Blossom.* The other, situated in the Katmai National

Monument on the Alaska Peninsula, was named by Capt. James Cook, RN, in 1778 in honor of Dr. John Douglas, the canon of Windsor. [*See* Barrow; Douglas.]

Duke Island (SEA). Two places at opposite geographic extremes of Alaska—Duke Island at the entrance to the Inside Passage and Prudhoe Bay in the Arctic Ocean—honor the same English family, the Percys of Northumberland. The island was so titled in 1879 by William Healey Dall, USC&GS, as an extension of the name of its southern tip, which Capt. George Vancouver, RN, had called Northumberland Cape in 1793 to honor Sir Hugh Percy, 1st duke of Northumberland. The duke was born Sir Hugh Smithson and received his title and surname through his wife's inheritance. His natural son, James Lewis Macie (legitimized as James Smithson), bequeathed over £100,000 to the United States to found the Smithsonian Institution. One of his legitimate sons, Sir Hugh, the 2nd duke, was a British general in the American Revolutionary War. His grandson, Algernon Percy, the 4th duke of Northumberland and 1st Baron Prudhoe, was the man honored by explorer Sir John Franklin in 1826. [*See* Prudhoe Bay.]

Duncan Canal (SEA). This Alexander Archipelago waterway was named in 1793 by Capt. George Vancouver, RN, to honor Scottish-born British naval hero and 1st Viscount Duncan of Camperdown, Adam Duncan.

Dundas Islands, DUHN-duhs (BC). The Dixon Entrance islands were named in 1793 by Capt. George Vancouver, RN, after Henry Dundas, treasurer of the Royal Navy, 1783–1800, under Prime Minister William Pitt.

Dutch Harbor (SWA). Site of a major USN installation attacked by the Japanese on 3 June 1942, this anchorage in Unalaska Bay was so named by the Russians because they believed the harbor was first entered by a vessel from The Netherlands.

Dutton (SCA). This ghost town on the northeast coast of the Alaska Peninsula was named by its first postmaster, mine promoter George W. Dutton, after himself in 1905. Mount Dutton,

on the southeast coast of the peninsula, honors USA geologist
Clarence E. Dutton, a nineteenth-century expert on volcanoes.

Dyea, DEYE-EE (SEA). Ghost town 5 miles west of Skagway
bears the name of a Chilkat Indian village originally located at
the mouth of the Taiya River. Dyea and Taiya are phonetic
adaptations of the same Tlingit word purportedly meaning "carrying place." Site of a trading post founded prior to the Yukon
Gold Rush by a former Montana sheriff, John J. Healy, the town
boomed briefly as the starting point of the short route to the gold
fields via Chilkoot Pass. [*See* Chilkoot Pass; Skagway.]

E

Eagle (IA). This Yukon River settlement, 6 miles west of the U.S.-
Canadian border, was platted and named Eagle City in 1898 for
the American eagles that nested on nearby bluffs. It came into
being in 1874 as a trading post called Belle Isle operated by
Moses Mercier in collaboration with Arthur Harper and Leroy
Napoleon (Jack) McQuesten. [*See* McQuesten.]

Eagle River (SCA). This suburb of Anchorage derives its name
from the adjacent river. It is one of nearly 100 geographical features and sites in Alaska having this faunal term in their official
titles.

Eagle Summit (IA). The highest point (3,990 feet) on the Steese
Highway is a viewpoint for the midnight sun at the summer
solstice in June. The name comes from the nearby creek which
was given a faunal title by prospectors in the mid-1890s. [*See*
Mammoth Creek.]

Edgecumbe, Mount, EDJ-kuhm (SEA). This volcanic peak on
Kruzof Island was called Montana de San Jacinto (Saint Jacinto

Mountain) by the Spanish, Gora Sviataga Lazar'a (Saint Lazarus Mountain) by the Russians, and Mount Edgecumbe by Capt. James Cook, RN, for either a similarly named mountain at the entrance to Plymouth Sound in England or for the earl of Edgecumbe. [*See* Mount Edgecumbe.]

Edgerton Highway (SCA). Side artery extending from the Richardson Highway's Willow Creek Junction to Chitina was named for Maj. Glen Edgerton, early-day member of the Alaska Road Commission.

Edna Bay (SEA). This community adopted the name of the adjacent bay which, in turn, was found nameless by the USC&GS in 1903 and given its present title without explanation. It was a common practice of U.S. government agencies to assign arbitrary names, often in some alphabetical sequence, to facilitate survey mapping and charting.

Eek, EEK (WA). Village on the channel extending inland from Kuskokwim Bay bears an adaptation of the Eskimo term *eet,* meaning "the two eyes."

Egegik, EEG-gi-gik (WA). Village and bay take their names from that of the river flowing from Becharof Lake to Bristol Bay, which stems from an Aleut word meaning "swift river."

Egg Island (SWA). A translation of the Russian title, Ostrov Iaichnoi. Many islands in Alaska have this name, some because of their shape, but most because they are egg-laden rookeries.

Eielson Air Force Base, EYEL-suhn (IA). Located 26 miles from Fairbanks, the base, constructed in 1943, honors pioneer Alaska bush pilot Carl Ben Eielson. A former officer in the Airplane Division of the USA Signal Corps, Captain Eielson started flying in Alaska on 3 July 1923 and chalked up an enviable record: first official mail flight in Alaska, 1924; flight over the North Pole, 1928; Antarctic exploration flights, 1928. He was killed in an air crash in Siberia in 1929 while airlifting furs from the icebound schooner, *Nanuk.* [*See* Wien Mountain.]

Eldorado Creek (YT). Purportedly one of the richest placer creeks in the world, this Klondike basin stream was named by members of the party of prospectors headed by ex-Chicago newspaper reporter John Williams. The name is that of the legendary "city of gold" sought by early Spanish explorers on the American continents and literally means "the gilded [one]." [*See* Bonanza Creek.]

Elfin Cove (SEA). This community is situated on a mile-wide cove on Chichagof Island that was initially known to fishermen as the "Gunk Hole," an East Coast term for a safe harbor having a narrow entrance. About 1928 Ernest O. Swanson built a salmon salting station on the east shore of the cove; and when a post office was established at the site in 1935, his wife, the first postmaster, discarded Gunk Hole in favor of the present descriptive name adopted from one of Swanson's harbor boats.

Elliott Highway (IA). The eventual "Road to Nome" now runs from Fairbanks through Livengood to Manley Hot Springs and is named for Maj. Malcolm Elliott, USA, president of the Alaska Road Commission when the highway's construction was initiated in 1936.

Elmendorf Air Force Base, EL-muhn-DORF (SCA). Situated near Anchorage, this USAF installation was activated in 1940 as the Army Air Corps flying field at Fort Richardson (prior to the separation of the USAF from the USA in 1947). The name honors Capt. Hugh Elmendorf, USA Air Corps, who was killed in an air crash at Wright Field, Ohio, in 1933. [*See* Fort Richardson.]

Elsa (YT). This silver mine community takes its name from a claim staked around 1900 by Charles Brefalt and named for a woman in his native Sweden. [*See* Keno.]

Endicott Mountains (AA). This range in the center of Arctic Alaska and Endicott Arm, a waterway east of Stephens Passage, are among the namesakes designated in the 1880s by officers of the USA and USN to honor William Crowninshield Endicott, secretary of war under President Grover Cleveland. [*See* Tracy Arm.]

English Bay (SCA). Community name is a translation of the Russian name applied to the Kenai Peninsula bay because it was initially charted by Great Britain's Capt. Nathaniel Portlock. [*See* Portlock.*]

Ernest Sound (SEA). Named Prince Ernest Sound by Capt. George Vancouver, RN, in 1793 for one of George III's nine sons. [*See* Prince William Sound.]

Eschscholtz Bay, EK-hohltz (AA). Named by Lt. Otto von Kotzebue, IRN, in 1816 in honor of the expedition's physician, Johann Friedrich Eschscholtz. [*See* Kotzebue.]

Eskimo Islands (AA). Named Esquimaux Island in 1837 by Hudson's Bay Company explorers Peter Warren Dease and Thomas Simpson. The word "Eskimo" is of Cree origination, meaning "eaters of raw meat," and was used by the Indians as a name for their neighbors to the north. [*See* Harrison Bay.]

Espada Point, es-PAH-duh (SEA). The west tip of San Clemente Island on the Portillo Channel was named Punta de Espada, meaning "sword point," by Capt. Juan Francisco de la Bodega y Quadra on his second voyage to Alaska in 1779. [*See* San Clemente Island.]

Ester (IA). Community name is derived from that of the nearby creek named for Ester Duffy and has been variously known as Ester, Ester City, and Berry. The latter name was that of a post office established there in 1906 which honored Clarence and Frank Berry, who mined in the area after Clarence Berry accumulated a fortune in the Klondike Gold Rush.

Estrella, Port, es-TREL-uh (SEA). This estuary on the west coast of Prince of Wales Island was named Puerto de Estrella, "port of the [North] Star," in 1779 by Francisco Antonio Maurelle, navigator for Capt. Juan Francisco de la Bodega y Quadra.

Etolin Island, e-TOH-lin (SEA). One of several landmarks along the Alaska coastline that honor Capt. Adolf Karlovich Etolin, IRN, who surveyed the Bering Sea, 1822–24, and served as governor of Russian America, 1841–45.

F

Fairbanks (IA). Alaska's second largest city was established in 1901 as a trading post on the Chena River by Capt. E. T. Barnette, who arrived on the river steamer *Lavelle Young*. With the discovery of gold by Felix Pedro in July 1902 on creeks 10 miles to the north, "Barnettes Cache" became a boom camp, and miners at a meeting in September changed the name to honor Indiana Senator Charles Warren Fairbanks (later vice-president under Theodore Roosevelt, 1905–9) at the suggestion of a political crony, Judge James J. Wickersham. [*See* Pedro Creek.]

Fairweather, Mount (SEA). Mountain and cape in Glacier Bay National Monument were so named by Capt. James Cook, RN, in 1778 because his expedition enjoyed good weather during the exploration of the area. Situated astride the Alaska-Canada border, the 15,300-foot peak is the highest point in the Province of British Columbia. [*See* Saint Elias Mountains.]

False Pass (SWA). Village on the east shore of Unimak Island gets its name from an early English misnomer for the adjacent Isanotski Strait believed unpassable at its northern end. [*See* Isanotski Strait.]

Faro, FAIR-oh (YT). The community name is that of a once-popular gambling game which a luck-seeking miner affixed to his claim on this site. The game's name derived from early

French playing cards bearing a stylized portrait of an Egyptian pharaoh.

Favorite Channel (SEA). The 16-mile-long waterway connecting Stephens Passage to Lynn Canal was named in 1880 by USN officers aboard the chartered steamship *Favorite* used for coastal survey work.

Fenimore Pass (SWA). This water passage in the Andreanof Islands, from the Pacific Ocean to the Bering Sea, was named by the USN in 1936 after the U.S.S. *Fenimore Cooper,* one of the ships attached to the North Pacific Exploring Expedition of 1855.

Fidalgo, Port, fi-DAWL-goh (SEA). Name of the fiord on the east coast of Prince William Sound honors Spanish explorer Lt. Salvador Fidalgo, whose launch party discovered the estuary on 14 June 1790. Just when and how the name was assigned is not known. The name was not on maps produced by the Spanish explorers Capt. Alessandro Malaspina and Capt. Juan Francisco de la Bodega y Quadra in 1791, but it was shown on the charts of Capt. George Vancouver, RN, as Puerto Fidalgo in 1794. As the two officers had previously met at Nootka Sound, it would seem that the British explorer either copied the name from Fidalgo's charts or named it to honor him.

Finlayson River (YT). Named by Hudson's Bay Company explorer-trader Robert Campbell in 1840 to honor Duncan Finlayson, chief factor and subsequently a member of the board of directors of the company.

Fire Island (SCA). Name of this island southwest of Anchorage in Cook Inlet between Turnagain and Knik arms is probably a translation of the Eskimo word *ignik,* meaning "fire." This term is also the derivation for "Knik Arm," and was used by the Eskimos as the name for the Indians living in the area. [*See* Knik Arm.]

Fireweed Creek (YT). One of several geographic features in the Northland with this floral name. The magenta-colored fireweed

(*Epilobium angustifolium*) is the official flower of the Yukon Territory and is so named because it grows in burned-over areas. [*See* Malemute Pup.]

Firth River (YT). This Arctic Slope river was named to honor a trader for the Hudson's Bay Company who resided 50 years in the Yukon and Northwest territories.

Fish River (WA). The stream that rises in the Bendeleben Mountains and flows to Golovnin Bay derives its name from the Eskimo term *ikathluik,* meaning "fish place." It is one of 3 rivers, 18 lakes, and 32 creeks in Alaska to contain the term "fish" in their titles. Among numerous variations of the faunal name are: Fish Choked Creek, Fish Egg Island, Fish Hill, Fishhook Junction, Fishless Creek, Fishnet Lake, Fishrack Bay, and Fishtrap Lake.

Five Finger Rapids (YT). So named because at this point the Yukon River divides into five channels. It was at the upper end of the rapids that Siwash George (G. W.) Carmack lived in a log cabin with his Indian wife Kate, an organ, and a collection of *Scientific American* magazines prior to his discovery of gold in the Klondike basin. [*See* Carmacks.]

Flat (IA). Mining camp established in 1910 and given the descriptive name of adjacent Flat Creek. In 1912 the town had a population of 400, and a dredge operated by Guggenheim interests recovered $440,000 in gold in 3 months.

Flaxman Island (AA). Named in 1826 by Sir John Franklin, RN, to honor the English sculptor, John Flaxman (1755–1826), who designed the white cameos on the blue background of Wedgwood ware.

Foraker, Mount, FOR-ay-ker (IA). This 17,395-foot mountain in the Alaska Range was named in 1899 by Lt. Joseph S. Herron, USA, to honor Senator Joseph Benson Foraker of Ohio. The early names of Foraker and McKinley mountains were often used interchangeably: the Russians referred to them as Bolshaia Gora or "big mountain"; the Tanaina Indians to the south and the Tanana Indians to the north apparently called both Denali;

while the natives in the area to the northwest who had a clear view of both peaks had separate names for each—Denali for Mc-Kinley and Sultana, meaning "the woman," or Menlale, meaning "Denali's wife," for Foraker. [*See* Denali Pass; McKinley, Mount.]

Forrester Island (SEA). Named in 1787 by Capt. George Dixon for Henry Forrester, steward aboard the fur trading vessel, *Queen Charlotte*. This Alexander Archipelago island was officially charted by Capt. George Vancouver, RN, in 1793. Vancouver and Dixon had been shipmates on the Cook voyage of 1778, the former a midshipman and the latter as a petty officer. [*See* Dixon Entrance.]

Fort Greely (IA). Established as USAF's Big Delta Airfield in 1942, the post became the headquarters of the Army Arctic Test Center in 1948 and, upon construction of a larger facility in 1955, was dedicated to the honor of Maj. Gen. Adolphus Washington Greely, Arctic explorer and founder of the Alaska Communications System. [*See* Big Delta.]

Fort Hamlin (IA). This abandoned trading post on the Yukon River north of Livengood was established by the Alaska Commercial Company and named in honor of Charles Sumner Hamlin, assistant secretary of the treasury, 1893–97, who was a delegate to the 1897 Anglo-American fur-seal fishing convention.

Fort Nelson (BC). As the site of a Hudson's Bay Company trading post around 1800, this fort was named for famed British naval hero, Lord Horatio Nelson. [*See* Muskwa River.]

Fort Reliance (YT). A former trading post established in 1874 on the Yukon River 6 miles below the present city of Dawson. Its founder, Leroy Napoleon (Jack) McQuesten, and his partners, Al Mayo and Arthur Harper, free traders for the Alaska Commercial Company, established a string of trading posts that played vital roles in the early search for gold in the Yukon. [*See* Circle; Eagle; McQuesten.]

Fort Richardson (SCA). Constructed in 1940, this post (including the Army Air Corps flying field now known as Elmendorf AFB)

was named in honor of Gen. Wilds Preston Richardson, first president of the Alaska Road Commission, who laid out the Valdez-
Fairbanks Trail that became the present-day Richardson Highway. With separation of the USAF from USA jurisdiction, the
military reservation was split between the Department of the
Air Force and the Department of the Army. [*See* Elmendorf Air
Force Base.]

Fort Saint James (BC). Established in 1806 by Simon Fraser, the
trading post was the New Caledonia headquarters of the Hudson's Bay Company. [*See* British Columbia.]

Fort Saint John (BC). Site of the oldest white settlement in mainland British Columbia, the original fort was built in the mid-
1790s by the North West Company under the direction of Sir
Alexander Mackenzie, first white man to traverse the area from
the Great Lakes region to the Pacific Coast. [*See* Mackenzie
Mountains.]

Fort Selkirk (YT). Name honors Thomas Douglas, 5th earl of
Selkirk and major stockholder in the Hudson's Bay Company
who attempted in the 1850s to resettle Scottish farmers in British
North America. The first post was established at the confluence
of the Pelly and Lewes rivers in 1848 by the Hudson's Bay Company explorer-trader, Robert Campbell, and burned by the Chilkoot Indians in 1852 to protect their trade monopoly with the
"Stick" Indians of the Yukon interior. The site subsequently
served as a trading post and settlement known variously as Fort
Selkirk and Selkirk in the pre- and post-Klondike Gold Rush
eras. [*See* Campbell Mountains; Colville River.]

Fortuna Ledge, for-TOON-uh (WA). Post office name for the
Yukon River community of Marshall. The gold camp, established as Marshall Landing, was named for Thomas R. Marshall,
vice-president in the Woodrow Wilson administration. [*See*
Marshall.]

Fort Wainwright (IA). Initially Ladd Field, an Army Air Corps
field activated in 1940, this Fairbanks post was transferred to USA

jurisdiction in 1961 and given its present title in honor of Gen. Jonathan M. Wainwright, the World War II "hero of Bataan."

Fortymile River (YT). So named because it joins the Yukon River approximately 40 miles downstream from old Fort Reliance. A miners' camp was established at the confluence of the rivers in 1886 upon discovery of placer gold by prospector-trader Arthur Harper. It was at Fortymile—now a ghost town—that the first claims on Bonanza Creek were registered, and from this point the news of the Klondike gold strike spread to the outside world. [*See* Harper, Mount; Sixtymile River; Twelvemile Creek.]

Fort Yukon (IA). Town at the junction of the Yukon and Porcupine rivers in the center of the Yukon Flats derives its name from "Fort Youcan," the original Hudson's Bay Company trading post established in the locale in 1847. The post, the first English-speaking enterprise in Alaska, operated on Russian America soil in violation of Russian sovereignty; but when title to the territory passed to the United States in 1867, the site was taken over by the Alaska Commercial Company. Also located in the immediate vicinity is the USAF's Fort Yukon Air Station. [*See* Fort Selkirk.]

Four Mountains, Islands of the (SWA). A translation of the descriptive Russian name for this group of volcanic peak islands. [*See* Aleutian Islands.]

Fox (IA). Former mining town north of Fairbanks derives its name from its position on the banks of Fox Creek—one of 26 creeks and 39 other geographic features in Alaska to contain this faunal term in their titles.

Fox Islands (SWA). Translation of the name Ostrova Lisii affixed to this group by the Russians. Reports by early Russian explorers, including survivors of the Bering shipwreck, indicated that many of the Aleutian and other Alaska coastal islands were heavily populated—some almost exclusively—by foxes. [*See* Aleutian Islands.]

Frances Lake (YT). Discovered and named by Hudson's Bay

Company explorer-trader Robert Campbell for Lady Simpson, wife of the company's governor, Sir George. [*See* Simpson Range.]

Franklin Mountains (AA). Named in 1837 by Thomas Simpson and Peter Warren Dease, coleaders of a Hudson's Bay Company Arctic exploration expedition, in honor of Sir John Franklin, RN, whose route of 1826 they were retracing. [*See* British Mountains; Harrison Bay.]

Franklin, Point (AA). Capt. Frederick W. Beechey, RN, named the cape for his commander, Sir John Franklin, on 15 August 1826—2 days prior to the date Captain Franklin named Beechey Point for his subordinate, with whom he had hoped to rendezvous. [*See* Beechey Point.]

Frederick, Port (SEA). Estuary at the north end of Chichagof Island was named in July 1794 by Capt. George Vancouver, RN, to honor Adolphus Frederick, one of the sons of King George III of England. [*See* Adolphus Point.]

Frederick Sound (SEA). Waterway connecting Chatham Strait and Stephens Passage in the Alexander Archipelago was named in 1794 by Capt. George Vancouver, RN, to honor Prince Frederick Augustus, duke of York and Albany and one of the fifteen children—nine sons and six daughters—of George III and Queen Charlotte of England. [*See* Clarence Strait.]

G

Gakona, ga-KOH-nuh (IA). This community at the juncture of the Gakona and Copper rivers derives its name from the Indian *gakatna,* meaning "rabbit river."

Galankin Islands, guh-LANG-kuhn (SEA). These islands south of Sitka take their name from one of the islets in the group called

Ostrov Galankin by the Russians, from *galanka,* meaning "brick stove."

Galena, guh-LEE-nuh (IA). So named when it was founded during World War I as a supply center for miners prospecting for galena or lead ore. The Galena airport, adjacent to the community, is a strategic airfield serving both the USAF and the Federal Aviation Authority.

Galiano Glacier, gal-ee-AN-oh (SEA). Situated east of Yakutat Bay, this glacier honors a Spanish naval officer, Dionisio Alcalá Galiano. As a lieutenant in the Malaspina expedition he explored Alaska waters in 1791, and returned in 1792 as the commander of the *Sutil* to explore North Pacific coastal waters. [*See* Malaspina Glacier.]

Gambell, GAM-buhl (WA). The major community on Saint Lawrence Island honors Mr. and Mrs. Vene C. Gambell, Presbyterian missionaries to the island, 1894–98, who drowned in the sinking of the *Jane Grey* while returning from a leave of absence.

Gambier Island, GAM-bee-er (SEA). This island in the Alexander Archipelago was discovered by Master Joseph Whidbey of the H.M.S. *Discovery* in 1794 and named by Capt. George Vancouver, RN, to honor Baron James Gambier, English admiral who captured Charleston, S.C., during the American Revolutionary War and served as a commissioner in the Treaty of Ghent in 1814 between the United States and England.

Gareloi Island, GOHR-uh-loi (SWA). The name of this volcanic island, a member of the Delarof group, is derived from the Russian word for "burning."

Gastineau Channel, GAS-tin-noh (SEA). Narrow water passage separating Douglas Island from the mainland at Juneau was named by the Western Union Telegraph Company in 1867 probably for John Gastineau, an English-born civil engineer who worked as a Canadian government surveyor in British Columbia during the exploration for the proposed Alaska-Siberia cable. [*See* Juneau.]

Geographic Harbor (SWA). Name of the bay in the Katmai National Monument honors the National Geographic Society which, since 1890, has sponsored many exploration and scientific research expeditions to parts of Alaska and the Yukon Territory including Saint Elias Mountains, Hubbard Glacier, Mount Katmai, Pavlof Volcano, Aleutian Islands, Bering Strait, Mount McKinley, Mount Logan. [*See* Valley of Ten Thousand Smokes.]

Girdwood (SCA). Name honors miner James E. Girdwood, who settled on the shore of Turnagain Arm in 1896.

Glacier Bay (SEA). A descriptive name assigned by Capt. Lester A. Beardslee, USN, in 1880, as the bay contains over a dozen tidal glaciers, including Muir Glacier. The Glacier Bay National Monument was created in 1925 and abuts the Alaska–British Columbia border on the north. [*See* Whidbey Passage.]

Glass Peninsula (SEA). Long peninsula on the east side of Admiralty Island was named by the USC&GS to honor Adm. Henry Glass, USN, who as captain of the S.S. *Wachusett* had surveyed the area in 1881.

Glennallen (IA). This community has a coined name formed from the surnames of two USA explorers, Capt. Edwin Forbes Glenn and Lt. Henry Tureman Allen. Glenn, accompanied by USGS geologist Walter C. Mendenhall, mapped the area from Cook Inlet to the Tanana River in 1898. Allen, an aide to the commandant of Alaska, Gen. Nelson A. Miles, trekked 1,500 miles through the interior of the territory in 1885. Both men later attained the rank of general and both are commemorated by geographic features in the Chugach Mountains to the southwest of the town. The Glenn Highway that runs from Tok to Anchorage is also named for Captain Glenn. [*See* Allen Glacier.]

Glenn Highway. *See* Glennallen.

Goddard, GAW-derd (SEA). Situated on Hot Springs Bay on the west coast of Baranof Island, this site was settled around 1800 by the Russians, whose name for it meant "sheltered curative hot springs." In 1908 the Sanitarium post office was established at the site, and in 1924 the name was changed to honor Dr. F. L. Goddard, operator of a local health resort.

Gold Bottom Creek (YT). So named by Robert Henderson because colors he panned from the stream led him to believe erroneously that when he sunk a mining shaft to bedrock he would find "the bottom like the streets of New Jerusalem"—solid gold. Henderson abandoned his initial claim for a richer one on Hunker Creek, a fork of Gold Bottom Creek, but ill health forced him to sell it for a mere $3,000. Since Henderson had steered George Carmack toward the gold-rich Bonanza Creek and the strike that started the Klondike Gold Rush, the veteran prospector was eventually recognized by the Canadian government as the codiscoverer of the Klondike Strike and was granted a monthly pension of $200. The award in part substantiated English-Canadian claims that Henderson, a Nova Scotian, and not Carmack, an American, really discovered the riches of the Klondike. [*See* Bonanza Creek; Carmacks.]

Gold Creek (SEA). The stream east of Gastineau Channel was named by Joseph Juneau and his partner Richard Harris, who made the Silver Bow Basin gold discovery in 1880. This is one of a proliferation of "golden" names that evidences the importance of gold to Alaska, Yukon Territory, and northern British Columbia. Among the English-language oddities are Goldbug Creek, Goldengate Gulch, Goldmoon Creek, Goldpan Gulch, and Gold Standard Creek. [*See* Juneau; Silver Bow Basin.]

Goldpan Gulch (WA). A miners' term that has been frequently applied to various features of the Northland topography. It refers to the slope-sided metal pan prospectors use to separate gold from rock and sand via a rotating, water-washing action that forces the heavy nuggets and "color" to sink to the bottom while sloughing away the unwanted material. [*See* Placer Creek; Rocker Gulch; Sluicebox Creek.]

Golovin, GAW-luh-vin (AA). The name is derived—minus an "n" for ease of pronunciation—from adjacent Golovnin Bay. The community was established as a trading post by John Dexter about 1890 and briefly boomed as a supply depot following the gold strikes in the interior of the Seward Peninsula in 1898. [*See* Golovnin Bay.]

Golovnin Bay, GAW-lahv-nin (AA). Named in 1821 for a visiting navy brig that was the namesake of Capt. Vasilii Mikhailovich Golovnin, IRN, who twice circumnavigated the globe, 1806 and 1817–19. Previously he had served in the British navy under Lord Horatio Nelson and Adm. William Cornwallis, brother of the general defeated at Yorktown by George Washington in the American Revolutionary War. [*See* Golovin.]

Goodnews (WA). A translation of the Russian name assigned to the bay in 1818 apparently in recognition of the receipt of some favorable—but unrecorded—information. The name again lived up to its earlier connotation with the discovery of platinum in the area in 1927.

Gordon (AA). This trading post on the shore of Demarcation Bay is named for its founder, Thomas Gordon, who arrived in Alaska from Scotland in 1888.

Gore Point (SCA). Southwestern tip on the Kenai Peninsula was named in 1786 by Capt. Nathaniel Portlock for Capt. John Gore, RN. Portlock had been a master's mate and Gore a lieutenant on Capt. James Cook's voyage to Alaska in 1778. When Cook was murdered in the Hawaiian Islands, Comdr. Joseph Clerke assumed leadership of the expedition and Gore took over as captain of the H.M.S. *Discovery*. When Clerke died a few months later, Gore succeeded to the command of the force and the H.M.S. *Resolution*. [*See* Portlock.]

Graham Island (BC). The northernmost island of the Queen Charlotte group was named in 1853 by Comdr. James C. Prevost, RN, captain of the H.M.S. *Virago*, to honor Sir James Robert Graham, first lord of the Admiralty, 1852–55.

Gravina Island, gruh-VEE-nuh (SEA). Island in Clarence Strait of the Alexander Archipelago was named for contemporary

Spanish naval hero, Federico Carlos, duque de Gravina, by Lt. Jacinto Caamaño, who explored the area under orders of the viceroy of Mexico in 1792. The same naval officer was undoubtedly the person honored by Salvador Fidalgo when he took possession of the region for Spain at Port Gravina, a bay northwest of Cordova, on 10 June 1790. [*See* Revillagigedo Island.]

Grayling (WA). This Yukon River community's name is that of a troutlike game fish common to Alaska fresh-water streams and lakes.

Green Island (SCA). This island in Prince William Sound was descriptively named by Capt. James Cook, RN, in May 1778, when it was free of snow and covered with trees.

Green Monster Mountain (SEA). Peak on Prince of Wales Island was so named because it was the site of the Green Monster Mines around 1900.

Grubstake Gulch (SCA). Name utilizes a miners' term describing the custom of providing a prospector with food and supplies in exchange for a stipulated share of any wealth he discovers. [*See* Goldpan Gulch.]

Gulkana, guhl-KAN-nuh (IA). This village was established as a USA Signal Corps telegraph station ca. 1903 and given the Indian name of the adjacent river, then spelled Kulkana.

Gustavus, guhs-TAY-vuhs (SEA). Community name is taken from nearby Point Gustavus at the entrance to Glacier Bay. The point was named in 1879 without a stated reason by William Healey Dall, USC&GS. A geographer with a penchant for subtle name associations, he was possibly prompted by historical fact. The site had been visited by the British trading vessel *Gustavus* three years prior to Capt. George Vancouver's exploration of 1794. Also, the majority of the settlers in the area were of Swedish descent and, as the point was situated across Icy Strait from Point Adolphus, which Vancouver had named after England's Prince Adolphus Frederick, Dall could have been honoring the prince's Swedish contemporary, Gustavus Adolphus.

H

Hagemeister Island, HAG-uh-meye-ster (WA). Name honors Capt. Leontii Andreianovich Hagemeister, IRN, who served briefly as governor of Russian America in 1818.

Haines (SEA). Initially this town on Lynn Canal was the Chilkat Indian village of Dtehshuh, "end of the trail." In 1878 it became a post of the Northwest Trading Company called Chilcoot. In 1881 a mission was established at the site by Rev. and Mrs. Eugene Willard who subsequently renamed it in honor of Mrs. Francina Electra Haines of the Presbyterian Board of Home Missions. [*See* Chilkat Pass.]

Haines Junction (YT). So named because of its location at the juncture of the Alaska and the Haines highways.

Harding Icefield (SCA). Name honors the twenty-ninth president of the United States, Warren G. Harding.

Harper, Mount (YT). This 7,000-foot peak north of the Yukon River on the east side of the Alaska-Canada border was named for Arthur Harper, who arrived in the Yukon Valley in 1873 and was one of a trio of traders who helped open the area for prospectors. [*See* Fort Reliance; McQuesten.]

Harriman Glacier (SCA). Glacier and fiord honor railroad tycoon Edward Henry Harriman, organizer and sponsor of the Harriman Alaska expedition of 1899. The 2-month-long, 9,000-

mile cruise along the Alaska coast hosted a scientific corps of 25 experts including Dr. Clinton Hart Merriam, chief of the U.S. Biological Survey and one of the founders of the National Geographic Society; Frederick V. Colville, U.S. Department of Agriculture; famed Indian photographer Edward S. Curtis; William Healey Dall, USGS; Grove K. Gilbert, USGS geologist; and conservationist John Muir, founder of the Sierra Club—all of whose surnames now grace Alaska topography. [*See* Dall Island; Muir Glacier.]

Harrison Bay (AA). The bay midway between Point Barrow and Prudhoe Bay was named during the Hudson's Bay Company's expedition of 1837–39, headed by Peter Warren Dease and Thomas Simpson, to honor the firm's deputy governor, Benjamin Harrison. An inlet and cove to the west are named, respectively, for the two explorers. [*See* Dease River; Simpson, Cape.]

Hart Highway (BC). Named at its opening in 1952 to honor the former premier of British Columbia who sponsored its construction, the road officially became the John Hart–Peace River Highway twelve years later. At its southern terminus, Prince George, it is the junction point for the routes from Prince Rupert and Vancouver; its northern end, Dawson Creek, is the starting point for the Alaska Highway.

Hawkins Island (SCA). This island in Prince William Sound has a name of unknown source assigned by Capt. George Vancouver, RN, in 1794.

Hazelton (BC). So named by Thomas Hankin, ex-employee of the Hudson's Bay Company who platted the townsite, because of the profusion of hazelnut trees in the area.

Hazen Bay, HAY-zen (WA). Name honors Gen. William B. Hazen, chief signal officer of the USA who organized Maj. Gen. Adolphus Washington Greely's expedition to the Arctic in 1881.

Hazy Islands (SEA). Presumably the name was assigned by Capt. George Dixon of the King George's Sound (fur trading) Company in 1787 and reinforced by Capt. George Vancouver, RN, his former superior officer on the Cook voyage of 1778, who entered it on the official charts. The Russians called the islands by a somewhat similarly descriptive name, Ostrova Tumannoi, meaning "foggy islands." [*See* Dixon Entrance.]

Healy (IA). This community was first a gold mining camp, then prospered as a station stop during construction of the Alaska Railroad, and is currently a supply center for the lignite coal mines that abound in the area. Over the years it has been known as Dry Creek, Healy Fork, and the current Healy—all derived from nearby Healy Creek.

Heceta Island, HEK-uh-tuh (SEA). This 46,707-acre island in the Alexander Archipelago was named by William Healey Dall, USC&GS, in 1879 in honor of Spanish explorer Bruno de Heceta, who charted the area in 1775 while surveying the northwest coast of North America.

Henderson Creek (YT). This stream in the Mayo Mining District honors never-rich prospector Robert Henderson, who is credited by the Canadian government as codiscoverer of the Klondike Strike. [*See* Carmacks; Gold Bottom Creek.]

Herschel Island, HER-shuhl (YT). This island, the northernmost point in the Yukon Territory, was named in 1825 by Arctic explorer Sir John Franklin to honor his friend, Sir John Frederick William Herschel, the famed British astronomer.

Hess River (YT). A mountain range and a tributary to the Stewart River derive their name from pioneer William Hess.

Hinchinbrook Island (SCA). Named by Capt. James Cook, RN, in 1778 for the family estate of John Montagu, 4th earl of Sandwich and first lord of the British Admiralty, under whose auspices Cook voyaged. Montagu's father was the Viscount Hinchinbroke, from whom the island's present name spelling derives. [*See* Montague Island.]

Holkham Bay, HOHL-kuhm (SEA). Habitat of the Sumdum

Indians, the bay formed by Endicott and Tracy arms was named in 1794 by Capt. George Vancouver, RN, after a town in his native England. [*See* Sumdum Glacier.]

Holy Cross (WA). The original post office name of Koserefski was changed in 1912 to the present name to conform to the title of a Jesuit mission that has been at the site since 1886.

Homer (SCA). This town, situated on the southwest coast of the Kenai Peninsula, was established by gold prospectors in 1896 and named by them for Homer Pennock, one of their own.

Hood Bay (SEA). A bay, and subsequently a settlement on Admiralty Island, in addition to Hood Point on Kupreanof Island were named by Capt. George Vancouver, RN, in 1793–94 to honor Sir Samuel Hood, one of the members of the Board of Admiralty who signed the sailing instructions for his 1790–95 exploratory voyage. Admiral Hood gained much of his fame for victories over United States vessels in the American Revolutionary War; but he was also credited as "the Englishman who won the war for the colonies" because of his failure to relieve Cornwallis' troops, which thereby forced the general to surrender at Yorktown.

Hoole River, HOOL (YT). Tributary to and rapids in the Pelly River were named by Hudson's Bay Company explorer-trader Robert Campbell after one of his Indian interpreters. [*See* Ketza River; Lapie River.]

Hoonah, HOO-nuh (SEA). This town came into being as the major village of the Huna Indians, a subdivision of the Tlingit tribe. Initially recorded as *hooniah,* the native term is said to mean "cold lake."

Hooper Bay (WA). The village derives its name from the adjacent bay which honors Capt. Calvin L. Hooper of the USRCS.

Hope (SCA). Located on the south shore of Turnagain Arm, this village was founded in 1896 as a gold camp appropriately called Hope City by nearly 5,000 miners responding to the placer strike on Resurrection Creek.

Hotham Inlet, HAWT-uhm (AA). Named by Capt. Frederick

W. Beechey, RN, in 1826 to honor Sir Henry Hotham, lord of the Admiralty.

Houston (SCA). Community north of Anchorage, established in 1917 as a station on the Alaska Railroad, was named for Congressman William Cannon Houston, chairman of the Committee on Territories that processed the Alaska Railroad bill in the U.S. House of Representatives.

Hubbard, Mount (SEA). A glacier and the 14,950-foot mountain on the Alaska–Canada boundary in the Saint Elias Mountains were named in 1890 by Israel Cook Russell, USGS, to honor Gardiner G. Hubbard, founder and first president of the National Geographic Society. The society had joined with the USGS in sponsoring the geologist's studies in the Malaspina-Yakutat area. [*See* Russell, Mount.]

Hughes (IA). This village on the Koyukuk River began as a riverboat landing in 1910 and was named for the contemporary governor of New York, Charles Evans Hughes. Gold-laden Hughes Bar upstream from the village bears the surname of an early prospector.

Hunker Creek (YT). The gold-rich stream in the Klondike River basin was named for its discoverer, Andrew Hunker, a native of Wittenburg, Germany. "Old Man" Hunker, a veteran miner who had previously prospected British Columbia's Caribou country, packed a copy of Gibbon's *Decline and Fall of the Roman Empire* along with his gold pan. [*See* Carmacks; Gold Bottom Creek.]

Hunter, Mount (IA). This 14,573-foot mountain in the Alaska Range got its name by mistake. In 1903 a New York City reporter toured the area and, as the junket was financed by his aunt, he unofficially named a peak 9 miles to the north after her. In 1906 a USGS cartographer erroneously applied the name of Mrs. Anna Falconnet Hunter to Alaska's twelfth highest mountain.

Hydaburg, HEYE-duh-berg **(SEA).** Founded in 1911 as the site of the centralized school system for Prince of Wales Island, the community derives its name from that of its original settlers, the Haida Indians, who migrated north from their principal residence in British Columbia's Queen Charlotte Islands.

Hyder, HEYE-der (SEA). The easternmost community on the Alaska mainland was founded in 1907 as "Portland City" as a tie-in to its location on Portland Canal. Because of name duplication, the Post Office Department rejected the title in 1915 and the present name was proposed by the owner of the Big Missouri Mine in honor of Canadian mining engineer Frederick Hyder, who had rendered a glowing report on the mining claim.

Hyland River (YT). This tributary to the Laird River bears the name of an early-day prospector who finally settled in the Telegraph Creek area.

I

Icy Bay (SEA). There are three "bays" in Alaska known by the descriptive name, "Icy." The northernmost is an estuary on the east coast of Southcentral Alaska's Kenai Peninsula at the terminus of Tiger Glacier. The southernmost is a bight (a wide-mouthed coastal indentation) adjacent to Icy Point in Glacier Bay National Monument that is now officially called Palma Bay after the name, Baia de Palma, bestowed on it in 1791 by Capt. Alessandro Malaspina. The largest Icy Bay is an actual bay located northwest of Yakutat at the terminus of Guyot and Malaspina glaciers. It was explored by Master Joseph Whidbey and named by Capt. George Vancouver, RN, of the sloop H.M.S. *Discovery* on 4 June 1794, and subsequent eighteenth-century descriptions of the bay indicate it was then largely filled with snow ice.

Icy Cape (AA). Point of land on the Alaska coast of the Chukchi Sea was named by Capt. James Cook, RN, on 15 August 1778, as the existing ice pack made it the most northerly position the British explorer was able to reach in his quest for a possible northern route between the Pacific and Atlantic oceans. A second Icy Cape exists at the entrance to Icy Bay northwest of Yakutat and is a USC&GS translation of the Russian name, Ledianoi Mys, assigned by Capt. Mikhail Dmitrievich Tebenkov, IRN. [*See* Saint Michael.]

Icy Point (SEA). Because of the heavy concentration of ice floes along its shore, this point in Glacier Bay National Monument was so named by Capt. Mikhail Dmitrievich Tebenkov, IRN. A second point of land in Southeastern Alaska, on the south shore of Douglas Island, has the same name. All in all, there are more than a dozen coastal and inland geographic features in Alaska with the descriptive designation "icy" in their titles. [*See* Saint Michael.]

Icy Strait (SEA). This water passage between Chatham Strait and Cross Sound at the northern extremity of the Alexander Archipelago is a translation of the Russian name, Proliv Ledianoi, published by the USC&GS in the 1883 edition of the *Coast Pilot*.

Igiugig, IG-ee-YAH-gig (SWA). Name of this village at the west end of Iliamna Lake is appropriate to its location in the Alaska Range, as it comes from the Aleut word *kigusig,* meaning "volcano."

Ignek Valley, IG-nik (AA). Name is from the Eskimo word for "fire." [*See* Knik Arm.]

Iliamna Lake, ee-lee-YAM-nuh (SCA). Alaska's largest lake, 60 miles long by 15 to 20 miles wide, bears the name of a legendary giant blackfish that supposedly inhabits its depths and bites holes in the natives' boats. The lake drains via Kvichak River into Bristol Bay. A village on the lake shore and a 10,116-foot-high volcano east of the lake on the coast of Cook Inlet also bear the mythical monster's name.

Indian (SCA). Name of a stream north of Turnagain Arm was assigned to this station by the Alaska Railroad ca. 1921. It is one of more than 40 geographic features in Alaska—from the Spanish Isla Indiada to early prospectors' Indian Grave Mountain—that contain some form of the term "Indian" in their titles.

Indian Mountain Air Force Station (IA). This air force installation near Hughes takes its name from its location atop 4,234-foot Indian Mountain, which the Indians called Batzatgla, meaning "obsidian hills." The peak's present name was derived from the river that rises in the Indian Mountains.

Ingra, ING-gruh (WA). Former settlement on Nunivak Island variously known as Ingra and Ingar derived its name from the Eskimo Ingeramiut, meaning "mountain people."

Innoko River (WA). This 500-mile-long tributary to the lower Yukon River bears an Ingalik Indian name of unknown meaning.

Isanotski Strait, EYE-zuh-NAWT-skee (SWA). The passage between Unimak Island and the Alaska Peninsula bears a Russian adaptation of the Aleut word *isanaq*, which denotes a "split." [*See* False Pass.]

Itsi Lakes, IT-see (YT). Lakes and the Itsi Mountains near the Ross River headwaters bear an Indian term meaning "wind."

J

Jackfish Lake (YT). So named because the lake is heavily populated with "jack," a local nickname for northern pike, a long-snouted, many-toothed game fish. Many other lakes and streams in the Northland bear faunal names attesting to their abundance of trout, grayling, whitefish, and the five species of Pacific salmon. [*See* Kluane Lake.]

Jackson Island (SCA). Island in Cordova Bay honors Presbyterian missionary Sheldon Jackson, who served as U.S. general agent for education in Alaska from 1885 until 1906. The Reverend Mr. Jackson first visited the territory in 1877 to set up schools and missions for both Indians and Eskimos; seeing that the natives' caribou herds were dwindling, he initiated a program of importing reindeer from Siberia, which thus provided natives with a food- and hide-producing industry. [*See* Teller.]

Jack Wade Junction (IA). Junction on the Taylor Highway—north to Eagle, south to Tetlin Junction on the Alaska Highway—takes its name from a nearby, and now virtually abandoned, mining camp named for a prospector ca. 1900.

Jago Spit, JAY-goh (AA). Name of the point on the Beaufort Sea's south coast honors Lieutenant Jago of the H.M.S. *Enterprise,* which explored the region while on a search expedition, 1851–54, for Sir John Franklin.

Jake's Corner (YT). Name of the settlement at the junction of the Alaska Highway (Milepost 866) with the Atlin-Tagish-Carcross Loop Road has two possible sources. The "official" version is that the community was named for a Captain Jacobson, USA Engineers, who supervised construction of that sector of the old Alcan Highway. However, local residents contend the title predates the Alcan Highway and takes its name from that of a Teslin Indian, Jake Jackson, who frequently camped in the area on treks to Carcross.

Japonski Island, juh-PAWN-skee (SEA). This small island in Sitka Sound derives its name from a Russian word pertaining to "Japanese," because it was occupied in 1805 by shipwrecked Japanese sailors.

Jette, Mount (SEA). The peak straddling the Alaska-Canada border in the Saint Elias Mountains was named by the USC&GS in

1908 to honor Sir Louis Jetté, a member of the Alaska Boundary Tribunal of 1903. A former Supreme Court judge, Jetté was lieutenant governor of the Province of Quebec at the time of the international boundary commission and subsequently was chief justice of the province. [*See* Alverstone, Mount.]

Johns Hopkins Glacier (SEA). Name of this glacier in Glacier Bay National Monument honors the university in Baltimore. [*See* Columbia Glacier.]

Johnson's Crossing (YT). The oft-printed version of the origin of this community's name claims that it honors a USA engineering officer who selected the site for the Alcan Highway bridge across the Teslin River. However, local residents contend the name commemorates a Teslin Indian, George Johnston, who operated a ferry at the site during construction of the bridge.

Johnstone Point (SCA). The original descriptive name, Cabo Frío, meaning "cold cape," assigned by the Spanish in 1779 was superseded in 1879 when George Davidson, USC&GS, decided to honor Master James Johnstone of the Vancouver expedition's H.M.S. *Chatham.* [*See* Alexander, Point; Davidson Mountains; Whidbey Passage.]

Juneau, JOO-noh (SEA). The Indians' summer fishing camp at the future Alaska capital site was known by an Indian name meaning "flounder creek." The first prospectors alternately referred to the camp as Pilzburg and Fliptown. In 1881 the USN sent in a detachment to maintain law and order and dubbed the boom town Rockwell after the unit commander. In the same year the postal service opened an office under the name Harrisburg. A miners' meeting on 14 December 1881 ended the multi-name confusion with a vote for the present title in honor of Joseph Juneau who, with Richard Harris, in 1880 made the discovery in Gold Creek that led to the Silver Bow Basin strike and establishment of the town. A French-Canadian, Juneau was born in Quebec, migrated as a child to Wisconsin (where his uncle

Solomon was one of Milwaukee's founding fathers), and then moved west to the gold fields of California, Canada's Cassiar Mountains, and Alaska's Panhandle. At Sitka a disappointed Juneau and Harris were steered toward possible gold in the Gastineau Channel region by mining engineer George E. Pilz. Juneau made and spent a fortune and died in Dawson, Y.T., in 1899 while operating a small restaurant in an attempt to build a grubstake for a Klondike prospecting trek. Juneau became the capital of Alaska in 1906 and in 1970 the seat of the City and Borough of Juneau (3,108 square miles), purportedly the largest city in land area in America and the second largest in the world. [*See* Silver Bow Basin.]

K

Kachemak Bay, KACH-uh-mak (SCA). Bay on the southwest side of the Kenai Peninsula on which the towns of Homer and Seldovia are situated bears a native name recorded by the Russians. The exact spelling of the original name is lost, and hence the source and meaning are clouded. The name could derive from an Aleut dialect term meaning "smoky bay," as coal seams once smoldered in the surrounding clay banks; or it could be an Indian word for "high cliff bay," describing the 1,100-foot bluffs that rim much of the 40-mile-long bay. The name in its present spelling is repeated on the North Slope, where it is an unrelated Eskimo name of obscured meaning.

Kadin Island, KAY-din (SEA). Island at the mouth of the Stikine River honors M. M. Kadin, a native of the Aleutian Islands who served as pilot of the Russian survey vessel, *Rynda*.

Kagamil Island, kuh-GAH-muhl (SWA). Name of this member of the Islands of the Four Mountains is an Aleut term of unknown meaning.

Kaguyak, KAG-uh-yak (SWA). Villages and geographic features situated on both Kodiak Island and the Alaska Peninsula bear names spelled "Kaguyak," all derived from similarly pronounced but different Aleut and Eskimo words. The original spellings of the native terms, and hence the meanings, were lost in Russian transliteration.

Kaien Island, KAYN (BC). The island on which Prince Rupert is located derived its name from an Indian word meaning "sea foam."

Kaiyuh Mountains, KEYE-yoo (IA). Name derives from *kaiyuh-katana,* or "lowland people," an Indian term for the natives living in the area.

Kake, KAYK (SEA). The community's name is that of the tribe of once-warlike Tlingit Indians which has occupied Kupreanof Island since prehistoric times. The present town is situated at the site of Old Kake Village, known to the natives as Klu-ou-klukwan or "the ancient village that never sleeps."

Kakhonak, KAWK-uh-NAK (SCA). This village on the southeast shore of Iliamna Lake bears an Eskimo name of unknown meaning.

Kaktovik, kak-TOH-vik (AA). A village on Barter Island and the lagoon separating the island from the mainland now bear the original native name for the island. Initially, the Eskimos called it Katoavik, meaning "place to seine [fish]," and the lagoon was called Akvakniakvik or "whaling place." While the original Eskimo name for the island was transferred to the village and lagoon, the island's new name, Barter Island, reflected the island's use as a native trading site. [*See* Barter Island.]

Kalgin Island, KAL-gen (SCA). Name is the original Tanaina Indian title of unknown meaning. In 1792 the island, in mid-channel of Cook Inlet, was appropriately named Isla de Peligro, "danger island," by Spanish explorer Dionisio Alcalá Galiano. [*See* Malaspina Glacier.]

Kalifonsky, KAL-uh-FAWN-skee (SCA). Summertime community on the west coast of the Kenai Peninsula was given a bilingual name: *kali,* for the "fish" clan of the Tanaina Indians, and *fonsky,* a Russian suffix.

Kalla, KAL-luh (AA). Abandoned Eskimo village on the Kobuk River originally called Kallamute, meaning "Kalla people."

Kalskag, KAL-skag (WA). Two villages on opposite banks of the Yukon River—Kalskag and Lower Kalskag—derive their names from the Eskimo term, *kaltkhagamute.* The root word is of unknown meaning; *mute* denotes "people," or the residents of the locale.

Kaltag, KAL-tag (WA). This community's name is of Indian origin and is believed to refer to a species of salmon that spawned in the tributaries to the Yukon River.

Kamishak Bay, KAM-uh-shak (SCA). A native name originally recorded by the Russians as Guba Kamyshatskaia, probably meaning "bay of little stones."

Kanaga Island, KAN-uh-guh (SWA). This member of the Andreanof group has an Aleut name of unknown meaning.

Kantishna, kan-TISH-nuh (IA). One of several gold camps that briefly boomed into being around 1905 in the McKinley River area. This ghost town's name stems from the Kantishna River which has been variously known by such untranslated Indian titles as Contaythno, Kantishana, Tutlut, and Toclat. The last name, loosely translated by Lt. Henry Tureman Allen, USA, in 1855 as "dish water," is currently spelled "Toklat" and assigned to a major tributary of the Kantishna. [*See* Allen Glacier.]

Karluk (SWA). This native name for the Kodiak Island community is apparently an abbreviated adaptation of the native word *kunakakhvak,* of unknown meaning, recorded by the Russians around 1800 as Carlook, Karlooch, and Karluta.

Karstens Ridge (IA). Named by Episcopal Archdeacon Hudson

Stuck for Harry P. Karstens, a member of the first party officially to climb Mount McKinley's 20,320-foot South Peak, 7 June 1913, and subsequently the park superintendent. [*See* McKinley, Mount.]

Kasaan, kuh-SAN (SEA). Community, peninsula, and bay on Prince of Wales Island derive their name from a pre-1800 Haida Indian settlement in the area that the Tlingits called Kasi-an, or "pretty village," because of its large number of ornate totem poles.

Kasilof, kuh-SEE-lawf (SCA). An Indian fishing village on the west coast of the Kenai Peninsula grew around a Russian trading post in the late 1700s. First called St. George, it eventually adopted the Russian surname applied to the nearby cape and river.

Katalla, kuh-TAL-luh (SCA). Settlement on the bay of the same name was established in the early 1900s following discovery of oil in the area southeast of Cordova. The name is an Indian word meaning "bay."

Katlian Bay, KAT-lee-an (SEA). Bay, river, and mountain on Baranof Island are named for the Tlingit chief who sold the land at Sitka to the Russian-American Company in 1799 and subsequently led the Indian attack against the Russian trading post in 1802. [*See* Sitka.]

Katmai National Monument, KAT-meye (SWA). Created in 1918, the largest unit (2,697,590 acres) in the National Parks System takes its name from Mount Katmai, which erupted in June 1912. Located on the Alaska Peninsula northwest of Kodiak, the reserve contains Mount Katmai and its crater lake, "new" glaciers, and the Valley of Ten Thousand Smokes, all of which resulted from the eruption. Katmai, applied to several geographic features in the locale, is an Eskimo name recorded by the Russians in 1828.

Kayak Island, KEYE-ak (SCA). Believed to be the Gulf of Alaska island visited and named Saint Elias by Vitus Bering,

IRN, in mid-July 1741. The present name was subsequently bestowed by Russians who fancied its shape resembled that of an Eskimo kayak. [*See* Steller, Mount.]

Kelsey Bay (BC). The Vancouver Island terminus of the Canadian ferry to Prince Rupert was named for the Kelsey family who settled the area in 1922.

Kenai, KEE-neye (SCA). Located on the river and peninsula of the same name, the town was established as Fort Saint Nicholas, a Russian fur trading post in 1791. The name derives from the Russian adaptation of Knaiakhotana or Kenaiohkotana, the Athabascan name meaning "non-Eskimo people," referring to the Kenaitze Indian tribe living in the area.

Kennedy, Mount (SEA). A 16,286-foot mountain in the Saint Elias range and the 20-mile-wide water passage between Chugach and Barren islands that joins Cook Inlet with the Gulf of Alaska are recent name assignments to honor the thirty-fifth president of the United States, John Fitzgerald Kennedy.

Kennicott (IA). This settlement in the Wrangell Mountains was established in 1906 as a camp for the copper mines of the Kennecott Mining Company, which was named after nearby Kennicott Glacier. The town post office also carried the erroneous spelling of "Kennecott." The glacier was named by the USGS in 1899 for Robert Kennicott, director in 1865–66 of the scientific Western Union Telegraph Expedition. [*See* Cordova.]

Keno, KEE-noh (YT). The community's name is adopted from Keno Hill, to which miners had affixed the name of a popular gambling game which, in turn, is an adaptation of the French *quine,* meaning "five winning numbers." The original Keno Claim staked by Louis Bouvette in 1918 was soon surrounded with diggings bearing similarly luck-tempting titles typical of prospectors: Roulette, Pinochle, Faro, Gambler, Faith, Hope, and Charity. Though the Keno-Elsa area boasts rich placer gold mines, it is one of the major silver-lead ore producers in the world. [*See* Elsa.]

Ketchikan, KECH-uh-kan (SEA). The outgrowth of a salmon cannery founded in 1886 on Kitschkin Creek, this town boomed as a mining camp supply center in the early 1900s. Now a major shipping and fishing port, the city and its harbor have been variously known as Kach Khanna, Kitsan, Kitchikan, and Kichikan, all phonetic spellings of the stream's Tlingit Indian name. The name is purported to translate figuratively to "eagle wing river," as the water breaking around a boulder at a waterfall along the creek's course forms the pattern of a spread-winged eagle.

Ketza River (YT). Named by Hudson's Bay Company explorer-trader Robert Campbell in 1843 for one of his Indian canoemen. [*See* Hoole River; Lapie River.]

Kilbuck Mountains (WA). Name honors Rev. John H. Kilbuck, Moravian missionary to Alaska, 1885–98 and 1921–22.

Killer Bay (SCA). So named by the USC&GS after a field team witnessed a fight between a whale and a killer whale in this Resurrection Peninsula bay. [*See* Whale Island.]

Killisnoo Harbor, KIL-uhs-SNOO (SEA). This bay on the west coast of Admiralty Island derives its name from a former Tlingit Indian village called Kootsnahoo. Missionaries translated the title as "bear fort." While *koots* means "bear" and *noo* does mean "fort," *noohoo* means "rectum" according to the U.S. Bureau of Education's Tlingit-English dictionary. The Indians saw the island—heavily populated with bears—as shaped like a bear, with elongated Kootznahoo Inlet as its stomach and digestive tract, and named the bay accordingly.

Kimshan Cove, KIM-shuhn (SEA). This small bay and a former mining community on Chichagof Island share a name of Chinese origin meaning "gold mountain." The mountain is the nearby Mount Doolth whose Tlingit Indian title means "abundance [of berries, fish, and game]."

Kincolith, KIN-coh-lith (BC). This community on Portland Inlet bears a native name meaning "rock of scalps" because Haida Indians returning from a slave raid up the Nass River once killed several slaves whose struggles threatened to upset the war canoes and then hung their scalps on the bluff.

King Cove (SWA). Community on the southwest coast of the Alaska Peninsula bears its founder's surname.

King Island (AA). This small island in the Bering Sea was discovered and named in 1778 by Capt. James Cook, RN, for 2nd Lt. James King, expedition astronomer. After the murder of Cook in the Hawaiian Islands, King was transferred to the H.M.S. *Resolution* as captain and subsequently helped prepare the expedition journal for publication. [*See* Norton Sound.]

King Salmon (SWA). This village bears a faunal name descriptive of the run of king salmon up the Naknek River from Bristol Bay.

Kiska Island (SWA). Name of this member of the Rat Islands was defined by the USC&GS around 1900 as a Russian adaptation of an Aleut word meaning "gut."

Kiskatinaw River (BC). This river, crossing the Alaska Highway at Milepost 20, bears a Beaver Indian name meaning "cutbank."

Kispiox (BC). Name of a settlement and a river is an Indian word meaning "hiding place."

Kitimat (BC). An Indian tribal name meaning "snow people."

Kitwanga (BC). This Indian settlement's name is a native word meaning "place of rabbits."

Klawock, kluh-WAWK (SEA). This community on Prince of Wales Island derives its name from a Tlingit Indian village, Thlewhakh, reported in the area around 1850.

Klinkwan, kling-KWAWN (SEA). This Indian settlement on Prince of Wales Island derives its name from the Tlingit term *linqoan,* which pertains to shellfish.

Klondike River (YT). The name of this Yukon River tributary with gold-rich feeder streams is an adaptation of the gutturally spoken Indian word, *thron-diuck,* meaning "hammer water." It was so named by the local natives, who pounded sticks into its shallow waters to support their salmon nets.

Kloo Lake, KLOO (YT). Lake bears an Indian name meaning "fish."

Kluane Lake, kloo-AH-nee (YT). The largest lake in the Yukon Territory derives its present title from its Indian name, Klooahnee-munn, which literally means "large fish lake."

Klukshu (YT). This Indian village on the Haines Highway just north of the British Columbia border is named for the adjacent lake, whose Tlingit Indian title means "last lake."

Klukwan, kluhk-WAWN (SEA). Situated on the Chilkat River southwest of Skagway, this village derives its name from a Tlingit Indian term, *klukquan,* meaning "always [i.e., old] town."

Klutina River, kloo-TEE-nuh (SCA). Name for this glacier-born river is an Indian word meaning "river with big head."

Knight Island (SCA). An island in Prince William Sound and a smaller one in Yakutat Bay were both named by Capt. George Vancouver, RN, to honor Sir John Knight who, with the H.M.S. *Chatham*'s commander, Lt. William R. Broughton, had been captured and held as a prisoner of war by the colonists during the American Revolutionary War.

Knik Arm, k-NIK (SCA). The estuary at the head of Cook Inlet derives its name from the Eskimo word *ignik,* meaning "fire," which the Eskimos used as the name for the Tanaina Indians living on the north shore. [*See* Fire Island.]

Kobuk, KOH-buhk (AA). This village is named for the adjacent river which the Eskimos called Kowuk or Kowak, meaning "big river."

Kodiak Island, KOH-dee-ak (SWA). The name of Alaska's largest island (about the size of Connecticut) derives from the Eskimo word *kikhtak,* meaning "island," which was altered by Russian fur traders to Kadiak and officially given its present form in 1901 to conform to local American pronunciation. Three Saints

Harbor, the first permanent white settlement in Alaska, was established on the southeast coast of the island in 1783 and named for a ship of the Shelikhov Company. In 1792 the post was moved to Saint Paul Harbor on the eastern end of the island by Alexander Baranov, new manager of the Shelikhov (later, the Russian-American) Company. Thus, the city of Kodiak—the oldest permanent nonnative community in Alaska—came into being, and it served as the headquarters of the Russian fur trade and as the administrative capital of Russian America until Sitka was founded in 1804. [*See* Shelikof Strait.]

Koidern Lake (YT). Lake and river on the Alaska Highway route between the Donjek and White rivers bear an Indian name meaning "water lily."

Kokrines, KAWK-reyenz (IA). Indian village and hills purportedly honor a Russian trader.

Kolosh Island, KOH-lawsh (SEA). The Russians named the island on the west side of Baranof Island with a term derived from the Tlingit word, *kaluga,* which originally meant "dish" or "platter." The Russians called the wooden labrets worn in the lower lip by native women of high caste *kolushki* or "little platters," and this word was then further corrupted to *kolosh.*

Koniuji Strait, kawn-YOO-jee (SWA). Name is a Russian adaptation of the Aleut faunal term *kunuliuk,* meaning "crested auklet." The strait, the two islands in the Shumagin group that it separates (Big and Little Koniuji islands), in addition to islands near Atka and Kodiak, are named for species of the black and white diving birds—auks, murres, puffins—that inhabit the cold seas of the northern hemisphere.

Korovin Island, KOR-oh-vuhn (SWA). An island and strait in the Shumagin group and a bay, cape, and volcano on Atka Island in the Aleutian Archipelago honor Capt. Ivan Korovin, who traded in the area in 1762.

Kosciusko Island, KAHZ-ee-YAWS-koh (SEA). Alexander Archipelago island was named by William Healey Dall, USC&GS,

in 1879, presumably in honor of Gen. Tadeusz Andrzej Bonawentura Kościuszko, a Polish engineer who volunteered his service to the American Revolutionary Army. [*See* Cape Pole.]

Kotlik, KAHT-lik (WA). The name of the village and river is an adaptation of the Eskimo word meaning "breeches."

Kotzebue, KAWT-se-byoo (AA). The town's name derives from the sound discovered and named by Lt. Otto von Kotzebue, IRN, captain of the brig *Rurik,* who searched for the Northwest Passage as part of a scientific circumnavigation voyage, 1815–18. Son of a famous German dramatist, von Kotzebue explored the south Arctic shoreline of Alaska in 1816 and named several features in the area for famous scientists and painters—Adelbert von Chamisso, Ludovik Choris, Johann Friedrich Eschscholtz—who participated in the exploration.

Koyuk, KOI-yuhk (WA). The village takes its name from the adjacent river whose name has many various phonetic spellings, but no recorded meaning.

Koyukuk, KOI-yuh-KUHK (IA). This Eskimo village and a river bear an Indian tribal name of unverified meaning.

Krenitzin Islands, kruh-NITZ-uhn (SWA). A group of islands in the eastern sector of the Fox Islands was named for Lt. Peter Kuzmich Krenitzin, IRN, captain of the *Saint Catherine,* who led an exploring expedition to the Aleutian Archipelago in 1758–69. [*See* Akun Island.]

Krusenstern, Cape, KROOZ-uhn-stern (AA). Named by Lt. Otto von Kotzebue, IRN, in 1816 in honor of Adm. Adam Johann von Krusenstern, IRN, the first Russian to circumnavigate the globe. [*See* Kotzebue.]

Kruzof Island, KROO-zawf (SEA). Name honors an admiral of the Russian Imperial Navy and was variously spelled Crooze, Kruzow, and Kruzoff until given its present official form by the U.S. Board on Geographic Names.

Kudobin Islands, kuh-DOH-buhn (SWA). Named in 1882 by William Healey Dall, USC&GS, to honor Lt. Andrew Khudobin,

IRN, who took part in Capt. Feodor Lütke's exploration of the Bering Sea in 1828. [*See* Seniavin, Cape.]

Kuiu Island, KYOO-yoo (SEA). Island in the Alexander Archipelago has a Tlingit Indian name of unverified meaning.

Kupreanof Island, koop-ree-YA-nawf (SEA). Name honors Capt. Ivan Andreevich Kupreianov, IRN, who served as governor of Russian America from 1835 to 1840.

Kuskokwim River, KUHS-koh-KWIM (WA). The second longest river in Alaska heads in the Alaska Range near Mount McKinley National Park and flows approximately 550 miles into the Bering Sea. The name is of Eskimo origin, but the meaning is not known.

Kustatan, koos-tuh-TAN (SCA). This summertime community on the north shore of Cook Inlet has a Tanaina Indian name which can be only partly translated: *tan* means "cape," but the meaning of *kusta* is unknown.

Kvichak Bay, KVEE-chak (WA). Bay and river bear an Eskimo name of unknown meaning reported in 1828 by Capt. Feodor Petrovich Lütke, IRN. [*See* Seniavin, Cape.]

Kwethluk (WA). The village took its name from that of the adjacent river, an Eskimo word meaning "bad river."

Kwigillingok, kwig-GIL-ing-GUHK (WA). Name of the Eskimo village on Kuskokwim Bay derives from a native root word, *kwiga,* pertaining to "river."

Kwinhagak. *See* Quinhagak.

L

Laberge, Lake, la-BARJ (YT). Variously spelled Labarge, Laberge, and Leberge, the setting for Robert Service's "Cremation of Sam McGee" was named for Mike Labarge. He explored the Yukon interior in 1867 for a proposed Western Union telegraph line from the United States to Europe via Canada, Alaska, Bering Strait, and Asia. The plan aborted with the laying of the transatlantic cable. [*See* Telegraph Creek.]

La Biche Range, la-BISH (YT). Mountains and a river that form the southeastern border between the Yukon and Northwest territories bear a French title meaning "female deer."

Ladd (SCA). This settlement on the north shore of Cook Inlet was a former trading post known as Ladds Station after the name of its operator, C. D. Ladd.

Ladue River (YT). Tributary of the White River that flows east across the Alaska-Canada border is the namesake of Joseph Ladue, pre-Klondike Gold Rush miner and trader who founded Dawson City. [*See* Dawson.]

Lake Minchumina, min-CHOO-min-uh (IA). A lakeshore Indian settlement and an airfield bear a Tanana Indian name meaning "clear lake."

Lamplugh Glacier, LAM-ploo (SEA). Name assigned by the USGS honors English geologist George W. Lamplugh, who visited the Glacier Bay area in 1884. He subsequently served as an employee of the USGS and the Geological Survey of Great Britain.

La Perouse Glacier, LA-per-OOZ (SEA). Glacier and peak in Glacier Bay National Monument were named in 1874 by William Healey Dall, USC&GS, to honor Capt. Jean François de Galaup, comte de la Pérouse, of the French navy, who explored the area under orders of Louis XVI. La Pérouse and both of his ships were lost in the South Pacific in 1788, but information on the Alaska portion of the ill-fated voyage reached France through one of his officers, Baron de Lesseps, who earlier had been sent home via an overland route. [*See* Lituya Bay.]

Lapie River (YT). Named by Canadian government geologist George M. Dawson for one of the Indian canoemen who was accompanying Hudson's Bay Company explorer-trader Robert Campbell when he discovered the Pelly River. [*See* Dawson Creek; Hoole River; Ketza River.]

Larsen Bay (SWA). The names of this bay on Nagai Island in the Shumagin group and of a settlement on Kodiak Island are misspelled tributes to Peter Larson, professional hunter and guide in the area at the turn of the century.

La Touche Island, la-TOOSH (SCA). Named by the Vancouver expedition for Admiral La Touche-Treville, French naval commander during the French Revolution and under Napoleon Bonaparte.

Lemon Creek (SEA). Creek and glacier near Juneau bear the name of John Lemon, who prospected the locale in 1879.

Levelock, LEEV-lawk (WA). Prior to the establishment of the Levelock post office in 1939, the community was known variously as Kvichak, Old Kvichak, and Livelock. The current name is purported to be the surname of one of the locale's early residents.

Lewes River (YT). This name initially applied to the upper reaches of the Yukon River above its junction with the Pelly River. It was named by Hudson's Bay Company explorer-trader Robert Campbell to honor his superior, John Lee Lewes, chief trading factor. [*See* Campbell Mountains.]

Liard River, LEE-ard (YT). This tributary to the Mackenzie River was initially given the French name Rivière aux Liards, meaning "river of cottonwoods," in recognition of the trees lining its banks.

Lignite (IA). This railroad station settlement derives its name from lignite coal deposits in the area.

Lime Village (IA). The settlement's name is adopted from that of nearby Lime Hills, so titled in 1914 by the USC&GS because of their limestone composition.

Lindeman, Lake (BC). Lake at the end of the Dyea-Chilkoot-Lake Lindeman trail of '98 was named in 1883 by explorer-writer Lt. Frederick Schwatka, USA, to honor the secretary of the Bremen

Geographical Society, the German organization for Arctic explorations that had sponsored an expedition by Arthur and Aurel Krause to the Tlingit Indian country in 1881–82. [*See* Bennett, Lake; Chilkoot Pass.]

Lisianski Peninsula, liz-YAN-skee (SEA). Eight geographic features on and around Chichagof and Baranof islands in the Alexander Archipelago honor Capt. Yurii Federovich Lisianskii, IRN, of the ship *Neva,* who explored southwestern Alaska in 1804–5. His cannon destroyed the Indian village of Sitka in retaliation for the Tlingits' capture of Baranov's trading post, Redut Mikhailovskii, in 1802. [*See* Sitka; Theodore, Point; Urey Point.]

Little Diomede, DEYE-oh-meed (AA). This U.S. island in Bering Strait and Russian-owned Big Diomede 2 miles to the west are remnants of a land bridge that once joined North America and Asia. [*See* Diomede Islands.]

Lituya Bay, luh-TOO-yuh (SEA). Bay, glacier, and mountain in the Glacier Bay National Monument bear a Tlingit name recorded, without definition, by the Russians as L'tooa and L'tua. It was also known on IRN charts as Port Frantsuzov or "port of Frenchmen," and whalers called it Frenchman's Bay. The last two names recall survey of the bay in 1786 by Capt. Jean François de Galaup, comte de la Pérouse, who as head of a French expedition searching for the Northwest Passage attempted to establish an exploration claim to northwestern North America for Louis XVI. La Pérouse, in command of *La Boussole* and accompanied by a Captain de Langle in *L'Astrolabe,* sailed from France in 1785, landed at Lituya Bay in June 1786, and then sailed south to Monterey, California. Both ships and all hands were lost in 1788 in the South Pacific near the New Hebrides Islands. [*See* La Perouse Glacier.]

Livengood, LEYEV-uhn-good (IA). Named for Jay Livengood who, with N. R. Hudson, discovered gold at the site on 24 July 1914.

Lodge, Mount (SEA). Peak straddling the Alaska-Canada border in the Saint Elias Mountains was named in 1908 by the USC&GS to honor U.S. Senator Henry Cabot Lodge, who was a member of the Alaska Boundary Tribunal of 1903. A leading Anglophobe of his era, Lodge was a Harvard University history professor prior to entering politics. [*See* Alverstone, Mount.]

Logan, Mount (YT). The second highest mountain in North America and the highest in Canada, the 19,850-foot peak in the Saint Elias mountain range was named in honor of Sir William E. Logan, first director of the Canadian Geological Survey. [*See* Saint Elias Mountains.]

Long Island (SEA). The elongated island lying between the southern extremities of Dall and Prince of Wales islands is one of a total of 12 Alaska islands—4 others also within the Alexander Archipelago—officially called "Long." This one, at 14 miles in length, is the longest of them all, and its title is a translation of the original Russian name, Ostrov Dolgoi. [*See* Dolgoi Island.]

Lower Post (BC). This descriptive name was applied to a fur trading post established on the Dease River in 1873 to contrast it from Upper Post on Dease Lake. The posts and others along the Dease, Tanzilla, and Stikine rivers were part of the traders' route to the coast and Fort Wrangell.

Lucania, Mount, LOO-kan-ee-uh (YT). The third highest peak (17,147 feet) in the Saint Elias Mountains—and in Canada—was named in 1897 by Luigi Amedeo Giuseppe Maria Ferdinando Francesco, the duke of the Abruzzi, Italian naval officer and explorer, after the Cunard liner on which he had crossed the Atlantic Ocean en route to Alaska and the Yukon Territory. [*See* Bona, Mount; Quintino Sella Glacier.]

Lulu Island (SEA). This island in the western sector of the Alexander Archipelago was named by Theodore Chapin, USGS, in 1915 for his sister.

Lynn Canal (SEA). Explored in 1794 by Joseph Whidbey, master of Vancouver's sloop, *Discovery,* and named by Capt. George Vancouver, RN, for his own home, King's Lynn, Norfolk, England. [*See* Berners Bay.]

M

McArthur Peak (YT). The 14,253-foot mountain in the Saint Elias range and the 204-square-mile game sanctuary are named for J. J. McArthur, one of the early members of an international boundary commission involved in establishing the U.S.-Canadian border between Alaska and the Yukon Territory.

McCabe Creek (YT). Halfway point on the highway between Whitehorse and Dawson is known locally as Midway, but bears a post office name adopted from adjacent McCabe Creek.

McCarthy (SCA). Former copper mining settlement at the south edge of the Wrangell Mountains takes its name from the creek which honors miner James McCarthy, who drowned in the stream in 1910. [*See* Kennicott.]

McGrath (IA). The town was named for Peter McGrath, who operated a fur-trading post at the site. McGrath was a merchant and fur trader in Circle City in 1899, then migrated to Nome and finally to the Kuskokwim region, where his post became the town and he became U.S. deputy marshal.

Mackenzie Mountains (YT). Watershed of the Yukon River, the mountains take their name from the Mackenzie River (the second longest in North America), which was discovered and descended in 1879 by Sir Alexander Mackenzie of the North West Company. [*See* Fort Saint John.]

McKinley, Mount (IA). The highest mountain on the North American continent was named in 1896 by prospector William A.

Dickey in honor of William McKinley when he heard the news of the future twenty-fifth president's nomination. Approximately four-fifths of its 20,320 feet juts above the surrounding terrain, so the two-peaked mountain has a greater foot-to-summit rise than Mount Everest. McKinley's two peaks are collectively called Churchill Peaks, a name applied by the National Park Service in 1965 to honor Sir Winston Churchill, British prime minister during World War II. [*See* Churchill, Mount.] The 19,470-foot North Peak was first climbed on 3 April 1910 by William Taylor and Peter Anderson of the Sourdough Prospectors party. The higher South Peak was ascended 7 June 1913 by Episcopal Arch-deacon Hudson Stuck, Walter Harper, Harry P. Karstens, and Robert G. Tatum. The six men's names are each commemorated by one or more namesake geographic features within the more than 3,000 square miles of the Mount McKinley National Park, which was created by an act of Congress in 1917. [*See* Alaska Range.]

McKinley Park (IA). This community gets its name from its location at the junction of the Anchorage-Fairbanks and Mount McKinley National Park highways. Its facilities include a post office, airfield, Alaska Railroad station, and park headquarters. [*See* McKinley, Mount.]

Macmillan River (YT). Tributary to the Pelly River was named by Robert Campbell for James McMillan, a chief factor of the Hudson's Bay Company.

McQuesten (YT). River settlement named for Leroy Napoleon (Jack) McQuesten, a Maine farmer, former Indian fighter, and Fraser River prospector, who arrived in the Yukon area in 1873. McQuesten, frustrated in his quest for gold, turned trader and formed a partnership with trader-prospectors Al Mayo and Arthur Harper. Noted for his generous credit to and grubstaking of early-day gold seekers, he was the founder of Fort Reliance and Circle. [*See* Fort Reliance.]

Malaspina Glacier, mal-uh-SPEE-nuh (SEA). Glacier north of

Yakutat Bay honors Capt. Alessandro Malaspina, an Italian-born navigator in the naval service of Spain, who surveyed the Alaska coast in 1791. Malaspina, in two corvettes built especially for scientific exploration and manned by a hand-picked crew and staff of scientists, undertook a 5-year cruise on orders of Spanish Minister of Marine Antonia Valdés y Basan, who hoped the voyage would surpass the achievements (and the resultant glory) of Britain's Capt. James Cook. Two lieutenants on Malaspina's survey of the Yakutat Bay region were Dionisio Alcalá Galiano and Cayetano Valdés, who returned to North Pacific waters in 1792 as commanders of the *Sutil* and *Mexicana,* respectively. Named by William Healey Dall, USC&GS, in 1874, the glacier is approximately the size of Rhode Island. [*See* Valdez.]

Malcolm River (YT). This Arctic Slope river, which heads on the Alaska–Canada border, was named by Sir John Franklin, RN, after British Adm. Pultenay Malcolm.

Malemute Pup (YT). A prospectors' name for a small creek feeding one of the tributary streams of the Klondike River. Both words of the name are frequently used terms in the Northland. "Pup" was the miners' name for feeder runs—often seasonal freshets—which they treated as separate streams since a miner was limited to only one claim per stream. "Malemute" is a native breed of heavily furred dogs used by Eskimos and Indians as sled and pack animals. An image of the dog is on the crest of the Yukon Territory's coat of arms. [*See* Fireweed Creek.]

Mammoth Creek (IA). So named because early miners unearthed from its banks fossil remains of preglacial mammals. Forks of streams, in this and other areas of Alaska, were all given individual names by canny prospectors to circumvent the law limiting a man to one claim per stream; they were thus legally able to stake several 500-foot claims on one gold-rich stream. [*See* Miller House.]

Manby, Point (SEA). Point at the mouth of Yakutat Bay was

named by Capt. George Vancouver, RN, in honor of Master's
Mate Thomas Manby of the expedition's H.M.S. *Discovery*.

Manley Hot Springs (IA). The original name, Baker Creek,
was first changed to Baker Hot Springs and then became plain
Hot Springs upon establishment of a post office to serve the Hot
Springs Resort Hotel built in 1907 by Frank Manley. A half-
century later, to conform to local identification custom, the post
office was given its present name.

Marathon Mountain (SCA). This Kenai Peninsula mountain near
Seward gained its name from the 4th of July foot races to the
top of the mountain and back to its base, which were first run in
1915.

Margerie Glacier (SEA). Named by the USGS to honor French
geologist-writer Emmanuel de Margerie, who visited the Glacier
Bay area in 1913.

Marmion Island, MAWR-mee-uhn (SEA). The name of the small
island off Douglas Island's Tantallon Point represents another
of the erudite and subtle name associations (similar to those of
Gustavus and Adolphus points, Cape Pole and Kosciusko Island)
perpetuated by William Healey Dall, USC&GS. In 1794, Capt.
George Vancouver, RN, had named Douglas Island and nearby
Point Salisbury to honor Scottish-born John Douglas, bishop of
Salisbury. Nearly a century later Dall, remembering the writings
of another Scot—Sir Walter Scott—tied in names from Scott's poem
about the Douglas clan (character, Marmion; castle, Tantallon)
to the geography in and about Canon Douglas' Alaska namesake.
[*See* Tantallon Point.]

Marmot Island (SWA). Because of the hordes of rodents that in-
fest the island, the Aleuts called it Uhnik, the Eskimos Siksik, the
Russians Ostrov Evrashka—all referring to "ground squirrel";
yet USC&GS map makers translated the Russian *evrashka* as
"marmot," an animal not found there.

Marshall (WA). Name honors Thomas R. Marshall, vice-president of the United States when this gold camp boomed in 1913. [*See* Fortuna Ledge.]

Marsh Lake (YT). Named in 1883 to honor a Yale University paleontologist, Prof. O. C. Marsh, by Lt. Frederick Schwatka, USA, who rafted the Yukon River from source to mouth.

Marys Igloo (AA). The now virtually abandoned Eskimo settlement on the Kuzitrin River was initially a boat landing where goods destined for mining camps upstream were transferred from steamer to flat-bottomed barges. At the site, an Eskimo woman named Mary held perpetual open house for weary travelers and served them food at all hours of the day or night. The miners called the village Mary's Igloo, incorporating their hospitable hostess' given name with the Eskimo word meaning "shelter." The apostrophe was later dropped from the official name.

Massacre Bay (SWA). Named around 1800, this bay marks the site of the 1745 slaughter of all the Aleut males of the Attu Island village by *promyshlenniki* when the natives objected to the rape and seduction of their women by the Russian free-booting fur traders.

Matanuska Valley, mat-uh-NOOS-kuh (SCA). Valley, community, and glacier all derive their names from the river that stretches from between the Chugach and Talkeetna mountains to Knik Arm of Cook Inlet. The name appears to be an Indian adaptation of a Russian word used to describe both the Indians of and the route to the Copper River. In 1935 President Franklin D. Roosevelt, through the Federal Relief Administration and the Department of the Interior, set up a New Deal agricultural colony in the fertile valley. The federally sponsored project, to be paid for by the settlers over a 30-year period, included 200 40-acre tracts with modern houses and the necessary farm equipment. In May 1935 the first contingent of colonists—67 families totaling 298 people, primarily from Michigan, Minnesota, and Wisconsin—arrived, and the Matanuska Valley Farm Cooperative was launched.

Mayo, MAY-oh (YT). Formerly a trading post known as Mayo Landing, this silver-mining community honors Al Mayo. One of the Yukon's pre-Gold Rush prospectors-turned-traders, the former circus acrobat became a member of the McQuesten-Harper-Mayo partnership that pioneered the Yukon River country on both sides of the border. [*See* Fort Reliance; McQuesten.]

Meares Glacier, MIRZ (SCA). Named by the USC&GS in 1909 to honor Capt. John Meares, a former British naval officer who became a trader and sailed Alaska waters in 1786–87 and 1788–89. His trading ventures and personality brought him into direct conflict with other explorers and were instrumental in fomenting the controversy between England and Spain over possession of Nootka Sound. [*See* Boca de Quadra.]

Medfra (IA). Name origination for this community southwest of Mystery Mountains is unknown. It was originally a Kuskokwim River settlement known as Berry's Landing.

Mendenhall Glacier, MEN-duhn-hawl (SEA). The 14-mile-long, 4-mile-wide glacier emanating from the Juneau Ice Field was given the Indian name of Auke by naturalist John Muir in 1879. However, in 1892 it was renamed by the USC&GS for the agency's superintendent, Prof. Thomas Corwin Mendenhall.

Mentasta Lake, men-TAS-tuh (IA). Community, mountains, and pass all bear an Indian name of unknown meaning, possibly from *mantas-na,* whose suffix means "river."

Merrill Pass (SCA). Pass in the Alaska Range used by bush pilots as the flight link between the coast and the interior was named in 1929 by the USCG to honor its discoverer, Russell H. Merrill, a pioneer Alaska aviator who disappeared in that year on a flight over Cook Inlet. [*See* Wien Mountain.]

Metlakatla, MET-luh-KAT-luh (SEA). Established in 1887 and named after Metlakatla, B.C., by Scottish lay missionary William Duncan, who moved 800 of the Tsimshian Indian converts from "Old Metlakatla" north of Prince Rupert to "New Metlakatla" on Annette Island after a conflict in religious doctrine with his

Church of England superiors. The original Christian colony founded by Duncan was given this native name meaning "a passage joining two bodies of water" because it was situated on Vern Passage, which joins Tuck Inlet with the ocean.

Meyers Chuck (SEA). Village and bay on Cleveland Peninsula bear the name of an early-day miner joined with *chuck,* the Chinook Jargon word for "water." Literally, then, the translation would be "Meyers' water."

Middleton Island (SCA). Emulating his mentor's policy of titling landmarks after persons controlling naval purse strings, Capt. George Vancouver, RN, in 1794 named this small island in the Gulf of Alaska for Adm. Sir Charles Middleton, 1st Baron Barham, comptroller of the British navy. In 1778 Capt. James Cook (under whom Vancouver had served as a midshipman) had named Controller Bay and Cape Suckling to the east for the contemporary naval comptroller.

Miles Canyon (YT). Named by Lt. Frederick Schwatka, USA, in 1883 to honor the current commandant of Alaska, Nelson A. Miles, famed Indian fighter and Civil War general. This Yukon River canyon became a watery grave for many Klondike-bound gold seekers attempting to shoot the treacherous rapids in make-shift green timber boats and overloaded rafts. Jack London, author of *Call of the Wild* and other romantic Alaskan stories, earned $25 a trip as a pilot on this stretch of the river. A glacier in Alaska's Chugach Mountains was also named for the general in 1885 by one of his aides, Lt. Henry Tureman Allen. [*See* Allen Glacier.]

Miller House (IA). Name originated in 1896 when Fritz Miller indulged himself with the luxury—and novelty—of a log cabin in an area otherwise devoted to prospectors' tents. The site was also alternately called Mammoth House, as it is situated on the bank of Mammoth Creek where the tusks and bones of preglacial Alaska mammoths, mastodons, and lions have been unearthed. [*See* Atlin.]

Minto (IA). The community title is from nearby Minto Lakes which, in turn, derive their name from the Tanana Indian word *min,* meaning "lake."

Minto (YT). Abandoned riverboat landing on the Yukon River was named in honor of Gilbert John Elliot-Murray-Kynynmond, 4th earl of Minto and governor general of Canada, 1898–1904. During the Klondike Gold Rush, hundreds of stampeders bound for Dawson were trapped by an early freeze-up in the Minto area; many died of starvation, others wintered over on starvation rations.

Mitkof Island, MIT-kawf (SEA). Name assigned by the Russians honors a Captain Mitkov.

Moller, Port, MOHL-er (SWA). Named for his sloop *Moller* by Capt. M. N. Staniukovich, IRN, second in command of the Russian exploration of the Bering Sea, 1828. [*See* Seniavin, Cape.]

Montague Island (SCA). Named by Capt. James Cook, RN, in 1778 for John Montagu, earl of Sandwich and first lord of the British Admiralty, 1771–82. Cook also named adjacent Hinchinbrook Island for the earl's family estate. [*See* Hinchinbrook Island.]

Monte Cristo Island (YT). Sandbar island in the Yukon River near Dawson, site of a gold stampede in 1897, was optimistically —but, as it turned out, inappropriately—so named by American prospectors after the rich lode in Washington State's Cascade Mountains.

Moose Pass (SCA). Mountain village on the Kenai Peninsula derived its name from the frequent right-of-way difficulties with moose experienced by mail carrier Anton Eide in the area in the early 1900s. Famed for the size and number of its moose, Alaska has 50 streams, 10 lakes, and 22 other geographic features—including Moosehead Rack bluff and Mooses Tooth peak—that use the giant deer's name in their titles.

Mountain Village (WA). So named because of its location at the base of the first "mountain" en route up the Yukon River from the coast.

Mount Edgecumbe (SEA). Name adopted by the present community on Japonski Island when a World War II Navy station was taken over by the Bureau of Indian Affairs as a native boarding school and hospital complex. [*See* Edgecumbe, Mount.]

Muir Glacier, MYOO-er (SEA). Situated in Glacier Bay National Monument, this glacier is one of several geographic features in Alaska named for John Muir, conservationist and founder of the Sierra Club, who extensively explored Glacier Bay and discovered the 350-square-mile glacier in 1879. The nature writer and exponent of national park development researched the Bering Sea and Arctic Ocean in 1881 and was one of the scientific corps aboard the Harriman expedition's steamer, *George W. Elder,* in 1899. [*See* Glacier Bay; Harriman Glacier.]

Mumtrak (WA). An adaptation of the native name Mumtrahamute, meaning "Mumtrah people," who were the Eskimos living on the shores of Goodnews Bay.

Muncho Lake (BC). Scenic pass and lake on the Alaska Highway bear an Indian name meaning "big deep water."

Murder Cove (SEA). Name assigned by a USN officer in 1869 because a party of fur traders sleeping on the beach of this cove abutting Admiralty Island had been robbed and killed by Indians.

Murphy Dome Air Force Station (IA). Situated northwest of Fairbanks, this USAF installation takes its name from a dome named, in turn, for local miner John Murphy. "Dome" is a descriptive term frequently assigned by prospectors to peaks and hilltops with rounded or dome-shaped summits.

Muskwa River (BC). Indian term meaning "bear." The name is also the official postal title of Fort Nelson. The Muskwa River bridge, Milepost 296, at 1,000 feet above sea level is the lowest point on the Alaska Highway. [*See* Fort Nelson.]

N

Nabesna Village, nuh-BEZ-nuh (IA). This Indian village's name derives from the native name, of unknown meaning, for the upper Tanana River, which now is in fact called the Nabesna River. The small settlement of Nabesna farther south on the river was so named because it was established as the camp for the Nabesna Mining Company. [*See* Tanana.]

Nagai Island, nuh-GEYE (SWA). Bearing a native name of unknown meaning, this island is possibly the one logged by Vitus Bering, IRN, as the burial site of one of his seamen on 30 August 1741. [*See* Shumagin Islands.]

Nahanni Range Road, nuh-HAHN-ee (YT). Otherwise known as Yukon Territory Highway 10, this summertime road runs from Mile 67 on the Campbell Highway to Cantung, site of the Canada Tungsten Mine, in the Northwest Territories. The name derives from the Dogrib (Slave) Indian term *nahane,* meaning "people of the west," in reference to the native tribe in the locality centered at the point where the borders of the Yukon Territory, British Columbia, and Northwest Territories meet.

Naked Island (SCA). This island in Prince William Sound was so named in 1898 by Capt. William R. Abercrombie, USA, an aide to the Alaska commandant, Gen. Nelson A. Miles, purportedly because Indians once found a demented native woman running wild on the island.

Naknek, NAK-nek (WA). Village on the east shore of Bristol Bay, the river by which it stands, and the lake in the Katmai National Monument bear a Russian transliteration of the Eskimo term *naugeik,* meaning unknown.

Nanook Creek, NA-nook (AA). North Slope stream derives its name from the Eskimo word *nanoq,* meaning "polar bear."

Napakiak, NAP-uh-kee-yak (WA). Eskimo settlement on the Johnson River 14 miles southwest of Bethel was first recorded as Napahaiagamute. [*See* Napaskiak.]

Napaskiak, nuh-PAS-kee-yak (WA). Name of this Eskimo village on the Kuskokwim River 6 miles south of Bethel is an adaptation of Napaskiagmute, derived from the native terms *napa,* meaning "wood," and *mute,* meaning "people." Until recently the village name was spelled Napaiskak.

Nares, Lake (YT). Lake connecting Bennett and Tagish lakes was named by explorer-writer Lt. Frederick Schwatka, USA, in 1883 for British Vice-Adm. Sir George Nares, Antarctic and Arctic explorer. [*See* Nourse River.]

Nass River (BC). This British Columbia river, flowing into Portland Inlet, bears a native name meaning "satisfier of the belly" because it was rich in salmon and candlefish, the mainstays of the Tlingit diet.

Near Islands (SWA). Westernmost of the Aleutian chain, this group bears a translation of the Russian name Ostrova Blizhnie and was so named because they were the islands nearest to Asia. To the immediate west of the Near group are the Russian-owned Komandorskie ("commander") Islands that serve the USSR as a radio and naval station. [*See* Aleutian Islands.]

Nelson Island (WA). Name honors naturalist Edward W. Nelson, U.S. Signal Corps, who explored the Yukon delta in 1877–81 and served 5 years as a specimen collector in the Baird Inlet area for the Smithsonian Institution.

Nenana, nee-NA-nuh (IA). This community, located at the confluence of the Nenana and Tanana rivers, shares with the river, glacier, and mountain an Indian name whose suffix, *na,* means "river" but whose root word has defied translation since the 1880s. However, the name is widely known; first, as site of Saint Marks Indian Mission; in 1916 as a supply base for construction of the Alaska Railroad; in 1923 as the location where President Warren G. Harding drove the golden spike completing the railroad; and more recently as the setting for the annual Ice Classic—sweepstakes on the day, hour, and minute the river ice breaks up.

Newhalen, noo-HAY-luhn (SCA). Names of this village on Iliamna Lake and of a river are the end result of American prospectors' attempts to pronounce the Eskimo word *noghelingmute,* meaning "people of the noghelin" river area.

Nichols Passage (SEA). Waterway between Gravina and Annette islands in the Alexander Archipelago was named by the USC&GS after Lt. Comdr. Henry E. Nichols, USN, who charted the area while in command of the S.S. *Hassler,* 1881–83.

Nightmute (WA). Village has an Eskimo name of unverified meaning. The first syllable has been variously recorded as *nicht, nigh, nigt,* while the suffix, *mute,* means "people."

Nikishka, nuh-KIS-kee (SCA). A name of unknown derivation—and sometimes spelled Nikiski—applied to at least three former Tanaina Indian villages and boat landings on the northwest coast of the Kenai Peninsula, which are labeled numerically as Nikishka No. 1, No. 2, and No. 3.

Nikolaevsk, ni-koh-LEYE-yevsk (SCA). Kenai Peninsula settlement founded in 1967 near Kachemak Bay by Russian expatriate members of the Old Believers sect of the Orthodox faith and named for Saint Nicholas, the patron of their church.

Ninilchik, nuh-NIL-chik (SCA). Founded as a retirement community for superannuated colonial-citizen employees of the Russian-American Company in the 1820s, Ninilchik derives its name from the native word *ninilchika,* of unknown meaning.

Nisutlin Bay, ni-SUHT-lin (YT). An arm of Teslin Lake with an Indian name meaning "quiet water," this bay is bridged by the longest overwater span on the Alaska Highway.

Noatak, NOH-ah-tak (AA). Name derives from an Eskimo term meaning "inland river."

Nome (WA). Prospectors established this Seward Peninsula city as Anvil City, after adjacent Anvil Creek, in 1898. A year later gold was discovered in beach sand and it became a boom-town home of 30,000 gold seekers. The city was renamed Nome in 1899 after a nearby point on Norton Sound, which got its name in 1853 when a British navy cartographer misinterpreted a chart notation of "? Name" and recorded it as Cape Nome. The original Eskimo name for Cape Nome was Ayasayuk, meaning "sheer cliff," while the Russians called it Mys Tolstoi or "broad cape."

Nondalton, nawn-DAWL-tuhn (SCA). Situated on Clark Lake, the source of the Newhalen River that flows into Iliamna Lake, the village has been variously known as Nondalton Village and Noondalty Village. The name is purportedly of Tanaina Indian origination; meaning unverified. [*See* Newhalen.]

Nordenskiold River (YT). Yukon tributary was named in 1883 by explorer-writer Lt. Frederick Schwatka, USA, to honor Baron Nils Adolf Erik Nordenskjöld, Swedish Arctic explorer and geologist. [*See* Nourse River.]

North Pole (IA). This community, incorporated in 1953, bears a commercial promotional name which is an outgrowth of Santa Claus House, a store that answers children's letters addressed to Santa Claus c/o North Pole.

North Slope (AA). Part of the Arctic Slope, the North Slope comprises the area of Alaska north of the Brooks Range, excluding the region south of Point Hope, that drains to the Arctic Ocean. [*See* Arctic Slope.]

Northway (IA). This village, 5 miles south of Northway Junction on the Alaska Highway, was initially a key link in the Northwest Staging Route of World War II. Its name honors veteran Alaskan

James A. Northway, steamboat captain, stagecoach driver, and
trading post operator.

Norton Sound (WA). Discovered in 1778 by Capt. James Cook,
RN, who named it to honor Fletcher Norton, 1st Baron Grantley,
speaker of the House of Commons and kinsman of the expedition's 2nd Lt. James King, later captain of the H.M.S. *Resolution*. [*See* King Island.]

Nourse River, NORS (SEA). Tributary to the Taiya River (Taiya
and Dyea are from the same Tlingit Indian root word) that heads
at Chilkoot Pass was named by explorer-writer Lt. Frederick
Schwatka, USA, in 1883 after a professor at the U.S. Naval Ob-
servatory. It was one of more than a dozen names of noted scientists of many nationalities—Swiss, French, Russian, Swedish,
and American—that the sycophantic officer affixed to landmarks
along his route to and down the Yukon River in 1883. [*See*
Schwatka Mountains.]

Novarupta, Mount, NOH-vuh-RUHP-tuh (SWA). Name mean-
ing "new eruptions" was assigned by the National Geographic
Society expedition of 1916 as descriptive of the volcano in the
Valley of Ten Thousand Smokes that had erupted in 1912. [*See*
Katmai National Monument.]

Noyes Island, NOIZ (SEA). The twenty-fifth largest in size in
the Alexander Archipelago, this 31,694-acre island was named in
1879 by William Healey Dall for William M. Noyes, a fellow employee of the USC&GS. A different Noyes—the onetime commandant of the Alaska National Guard and director of the
Alaska Road Commission, Gen. John R. Noyes—is honored by
a namesake peak in the Mentasta Mountains.

Nugget Gulch (IA). Name is a prospectors' term descriptive of
the object of their search. "Nugget" means a lump of native gold,
while "color" is a particle of the mineral which miners take as an
indication of the presence of gold in the prospect. [*See* Goldpan
Gulch.]

Nuka Island, NOO-kuh (SCA). Island and nearby bay off the

Kenai Peninsula bear a Russian derivative of the Eskimo word *nukaq,* meaning "young bull caribou."

Nulato, noo-LAH-toh (IA). Community name comes from that of the tributary to the Yukon River which in the Koyukon dialect of Athabascan spoken by the Nulato Indians meant "place where the dog [chum] salmon come." It was a traditional native trading site where interior Indians bartered with coast Eskimos for items that came from the Chukchi tribesmen of Siberia. A Russian trading post was established in the immediate locale in 1838 and burned out by the Koyukons in 1838, 1839, and 1851. In the last attack virtually everyone in the post was massacred—Indian workers, Creoles, Russians, and a Lt. John J. Bernard, RN, of the H.M.S. *Enterprise,* who was on an inland quest for information concerning missing English explorer Sir John Franklin. [*See* Anvik.]

Nunivak Island, NOO-nuh-VAK (WA). Bering Sea island separated from the mainland by Etolin Strait bears an adaptation of an Eskimo term meaning "big land."

Nushagak Bay, NOO-shuh-gak (WA). Bay and other geographic features in the immediate area derive their names from that of the river, whose Eskimo title of unknown meaning was reported by the Russians as Nushegak ca. 1800.

Nutzotin Mountains, noo-TZOH-tuhn (IA). Range north of the Saint Elias Mountains is named for the Indian tribe that resided in the area.

O

Ogilvie Mountains (YT). Named in honor of surveyor William Ogilvie who (with geologist George M. Dawson) established the basic boundary line between Canada and Alaska in 1887, and who, as dominion land surveyor at Fortymile, made official realignment of the townsite of Dawson (City) and the haphazardly staked claims on Bonanza and Eldorado creeks. [*See* Dawson Creek.]

Oglala Pass, OH-glah-luh (SWA). Waterway between Rat and Amchitka islands was named in 1935 for USN survey vessel U.S.S. *Oglala,* which bore an Indian name for one of the Sioux tribes of the Dakotas.

Old Crow (YT). An early white man's adaptation of Te-Trhim-Gevtik, meaning "raven may I walk," the name of a revered chief that local Indians had applied to the region.

Old Harbor (SWA). Name of this town on Kodiak Island describes its location on historic Three Saints Harbor, site of the first permanent Russian settlement in Alaska. [*See* Three Saints Harbor.]

Ophir, OH-fer (IA). Settlement northwest of McGrath took its name in 1908 from a nearby placer creek—one of a dozen streams in Alaska to be named by Bible-reading prospectors for the lost country of Ophir, the source of King Solomon's gold.

Orca Bay, OR-kuh (SCA). The bay on which Cordova stands was initially called Puerto Cordova in 1790 by Spanish explorer Lt. Salvador Fidalgo. The namesake—one of several along the Alaska–British Columbia coast—honored Antonio María Bucareli y Ursúa Henestrosa Lasso de la Vega Villacis y Cordova, viceroy of Mexico during the Bodega y Quadra expeditions of the 1770s. [*See* Bucareli Bay.] Because of confusion with a similarly named bay at Dixon Entrance, a name change was approved by the U.S. Board on Geographic Names at the request of the USC&GS in 1906. The new title was borrowed from nearby Orca Inlet, site of the Orca Cannery operated by the Pacific Steam Whaling Company and appropriately named after the firm's vessel *Orca,* which is the species name of the *Orcinus orca,* or killer whale. [*See* Cordova.]

Orville, Mount (SEA). This peak in Glacier Bay National Monument was named by former Alaska governor and senator Ernest Gruening to honor Orville Wright, airplane inventor, in recognition of aviation's importance in Alaska. [*See* Wilbur, Mount.]

Oscarville (WA). Community south of Bethel was established as a trading post in the early 1900s by Oscar Samuelson.

Otter Island (WA). The island's title is one example of the frequent use of this faunal name in Alaska's coastal areas. The usage is appropriate, as it was the quest for highly prized sea otter pelts that led Russian, then English and American, hunters and traders to explore much of the region. While these adventurers' efforts were financially rewarding and enhanced the geographic knowledge of mankind, they were also criminally devastating: the native Aleut population decreased from 30,000 to a scant 2,000 and the otter count was cut from millions to virtual extinction. [*See* Bobrof Island.]

Ouzinkie, oo-ZING-kee (SWA). Name of this community on Spruce Island is an adaptation of *uzen'kii,* a Russian word meaning "rather narrow." Narrow Strait, on which Ouzinkie is located, is the present name of the passage between Spruce and Kodiak islands.

P

Palmer (SCA). Town was established as a station on the Alaska Railroad in 1916 and became the trade center of the agriculturally rich Matanuska Valley in the 1930s. The name presumably honors George Palmer, a trader in the locale in the 1880s. [*See* Matanuska Valley.]

Pastol Bay, PAS-tuhl (SWA). Bay on the southeastern shore of

Norton Sound, variously known as Pastoli, Pastolik, and Pastole prior to 1900, was presumably named for an early trader in the area.

Pauloff Harbor (SWA). Name is a recent phonetic Americanization of Pavlof Harbor, on which this community is located. In turn, "Pavlof" is based on the Russian name Pavel or "Paul." [*See* Pavlof Islands.]

Pavlof Islands (SWA). This frequently repeated name in Alaska geography comes from Pavel, the Russian equivalent for Paul.

Paxson (IA). Community at the junction of the Richardson and Denali highways derived its name from Paxson's Roadhouse established by pioneer mail carrier (Valdez to Eagle) Alvin J. Paxson ca. 1900.

Peace River (BC). A translation of the Indian name Unchaga affixed to the river by plains tribes to the east when they settled a territorial war at Peace Point on the riverbank near Lake Athabasca in the late 1700s.

Pedro Bay, PAY-droh (SCA). The village name derives from its location on Pedro Bay on the east shore of Iliamna Lake.

Pedro Creek, PEE-droh (IA). Stream near Fairbanks honors Italian-born Felix Pedro (Felice Pedrone), whose discovery of gold in the creek in July 1902 sparked the transformation of "Barnettes Cache" into the city of Fairbanks. Pedro also found gold on Cleary Creek, which was named for Frank J. Cleary, the brother-in-law of Capt. E. T. Barnette, who carried Pedro's filing notices to Circle City. [*See* Fairbanks.]

Pelican (SEA). This Chichagof Island community was named for *The Pelican,* a fishing boat owned by the settlement's founder, Kalle Raatikainen.

Pelly Crossing (YT). Community name is derived from that of the river, which was named by Hudson's Bay Company explorer-trader Robert Campbell in 1840 to honor Sir John Henry Pelly, governor of the company.

Peril Strait (SEA). Water passage separating Chichagof and

Baranof islands was so named by the Russians because 150 of their Aleut "employees" died from eating poisonous mussels gathered along its shores.

Perryville (SWA). Name honors Lt. Comdr. K. W. Perry of the USRCS vessel, *Manning,* who rescued refugees fleeing from the June 1912 eruption of Mount Katmai. The ex-residents of the destroyed village of Katmai settled in the area where the captain landed them and named their new home for him.

Petersburg (SEA). This town on Wrangell Narrows is named for Peter Buschmann, who established a cannery and sawmill at the townsite in 1897.

Petersville (SCA). Established as a mining camp, this community takes its name from Peters Creek, on which it is located.

Philip Smith Mountains (AA). Name, assigned in 1950 by the USGS, honors the chief Alaska geologist for the geological survey, 1925–46.

Pilot Point (SWA). Initially known as Pilots Station, the base for Ugashik River pilots, this community was renamed with the establishment of a post office in 1933.

Pilot Station (AA). This Yukon River community was named as a landmark guide by early riverboat pilots.

Pingaluk River, PING-guh-luhk (IA). This Eskimo name means "bad hill." Variations of the Eskimo term *pingo* are prevalent throughout northern Alaska, as it describes a large mound raised by action of the permafrost.

Pittman (SCA). Locality west of Palmer, established in 1917 as a station on the Alaska Railroad, was named for Nevada Senator Key Pittman, who actively supported the Alaska Railroad bill in the U.S. Senate. A native of Vicksburg, Mississippi, he was a practicing lawyer in Nome and Seattle prior to establishing permanent residence in Tonopah, Nevada, in 1901.

Placer Creek (IA). A name frequently assigned by miners, "placer" refers to deposits of gold in gravel and/or the process of removing the gold via water action rather than the crushing and chemical processing of ore. [*See* Goldpan Gulch; Rocker Gulch; Sluicebox Creek.]

Platinum (WA) So named because of platinum discoveries made in the locale in 1927. In 1937 the community was a "white gold" boom town.

Point Baker (SEA). Settlement situated on an offshore island in Sumner Strait takes its name from the nearby northwestern extremity of Prince of Wales Island. The tip of the island was named in 1793 by Capt. George Vancouver, RN, to honor Lt. Joseph Baker of the H.M.S. *Discovery,* who prepared the charts detailing the expedition's exploration voyage. The USC&GS and USN created topographical confusion when they joined forces to assign a reverse version of the title, Baker Point, to the east coast of Prince of Wales Island. William Healey Dall, USC&GS gave the name Baker Inlet in 1880 to a nonexistent cove on Kasaan Bay. Five years later, Lt. Comdr. Richardson Clover, USN, surveyed the area and came up a bay short and a name long, so he arbitrarily reassigned the surplus Baker to a small point in Kasaan Bay in honor of government cartographer Marcus Baker. This Baker had previously been honored by his associate Dall with a namesake island due west 45 miles. [*See* Baker Island.]

Point Barrow. *See* Barrow.

Point Hope (AA). This Eskimo village on the Chukchi Sea coast derives its name from its location on Point Hope which, in turn, was named on 2 August 1826 by Capt. Frederick W. Beechey, RN, to honor a friend, Sir William Johnstone Hope, of a British seafaring family.

Polychrome Pass (IA). A mountain and glacier derive their names from this pass between the two forks of the Tolkat River in Mount McKinley National Park. The descriptive name, predating establishment of the park, means "many varied colors."

Poperechnoi Island, PAWP-er-ECH-noi (SWA). Name of this island in the Pavlof group is a Russian word meaning "crosswise."

Popof Island (SWA). This island in the Shumagin group bears a Russian surname, possibly that of Vasilii and Ivan Popov, pelt hunters and fur traders who headquartered in the area in the early 1760s.

Porcupine Islands (SCA). One of three dozen geographic features in Alaska to bear this faunal name, the islands were so named around 1900 by the USC&GS because one of the group was a tree-studded hump that resembled a porcupine.

Porcupine River (YT). This border-traversing tributary of the Yukon River was so named by Hudson's Bay Company trappers in the 1800s because of the porcupine population along its banks.

Portage (SCA). This village at the head of Turnagain Arm was probably so named because it was on the portage route between Prince William Sound and Turnagain Arm, as was Portage Glacier to the south.

Port Alcan (IA). The name of this U.S. Customs and Immigration station is descriptive of its location at the international boundary between the United States and Canada on the Alaska Highway. The 24-hour-a-day offices are one-half mile west of the actual Alaska-Yukon border—Milepost 1221.8 northwest of Dawson Creek or Milepost 298.7 southeast of Fairbanks. [*See* Beaver Creek.]

Port Alexander (SEA). The name of this community at the southern tip of Baranof Island honors Alexander Andreevich Baranov, who served in the dual capacity of general manager of the Russian-American Company and governor of Russian America from 1799 to 1818. Although separated from Sitka by 60 roadless miles, the settlement is a part of the Greater Sitka Borough (the Alaska equivalent of a county).

Port Alsworth (SCA). Formerly known by the names Tanalian and Tanalian Point, the community on Lake Clark adopted its present name when a post office was established in 1950. The name comes from that of veteran bush pilot Babe Alsworth who, with his wife Mary, operates the settlement's trading post and post office. [*See* Clark, Lake; Tanalian River.]

Port Ashton (SCA). Community on Evans Island in Prince William Sound was originally called Sawmill Bay. The settlement adopted its present name with the establishment in 1918 of a fish processing station by Capt. Ashton Brooks.

Port Chilkoot (SEA). This community on Chilkoot Inlet was established in 1904 by the USA as Fort William H. Seward. The name honoring the purchaser of Alaska was changed to Chilkoot Barracks in 1922 as a geographic tie-in to the Tlingit Indian tribe living in the area. In 1943 the post was abandoned and four years later was purchased by World War II veterans who gave the fledgling town its present site and name.

Port Graham (SCA). Village takes its name from the bay at the southwest end of the Kenai Peninsula which, in turn, has been adapted from Grahams Harbour, the name assigned by Capt. Nathaniel Portlock in 1786. [*See* Portlock.]

Port Heiden, HEYE-duhn (SWA). Community takes its name from that of the bay on which it is located. The name initially assigned by Capt. Feodor Petrovich Lütke, IRN, in 1828 was Baie Compte Heyden for a "Count Heiden." [*See* Seniavin, Cape.]

Portillo Channel, por-TIL-loh (SEA). A translation of the original name, Canal de Portillo, assigned by Spanish navigator Francisco Antonio Maurelle during his second voyage to Alaska, 1779, to honor prominent José de Portillo, eventual minister of the Council of the Indies in Spain.

Portland Canal (SEA). Named 15 August 1793 by Capt. George Vancouver, RN, for the two-time prime minister of England, William Henry Cavendish Bentinck, the 3rd duke of Portland. The canal's mid-channel was set as the Canada-Alaska border by the boundary commission of 1903.

Port Lions (SWA). Town on the north coast of Kodiak Island was named in 1964 to honor the 49th District Club of Lions In-

ternational, which built the new community for residents of Afognak after their village was virtually destroyed by an earthquake
and resultant tidal wave on 27 March 1964. The terrain in the
locality of the former townsite at the south tip of Afognak Island
dropped 5 feet, and the residents voted to move to a safer area
on the larger island to the south. [*See* Afognak Island.]

Portlock (SCA). Former cannery town at the end of the Kenai
Peninsula was named for Capt. Nathaniel Portlock of the *King
George* who, with Capt. George Dixon of the *Queen Charlotte,*
explored the coast in 1786–87 while trading fur otter pelts. Port-
lock had been master's mate on Capt. James Cook's voyage to
Alaska in 1779, and the experience resulted in his return to the
area in charge of the two-vessel operation for the King George's
Sound Company. A glacier on the peninsula and a harbor on
Chichagof Island in the Alexander Archipelago also honor him.
[*See* Dixon Entrance.]

Port Simpson (BC). Name honors Capt. Aemilius Simpson (step-
cousin of Sir George Simpson, governor of the Hudson's Bay
Company), who founded, and later died at, a company trading
post in the area in 1831.

Port Wakefield (SWA). This Kodiak Island community, relo-
cated from nearby Raspberry Island following the settlement's
devastation by the March 1964 earthquake, was named for pioneer
Alaska entrepreneur Lee Howard Wakefield, who operated a
fish processing plant at the original site. [*See* Port Lions.]

Possession, Point (SCA). So named by Capt. James Cook, RN,
to mark the site where he claimed possession of the land in the
name of George III, King of England, on 1 June 1778.

Pribilof Islands, PRIB-uh-lawf (WA). Famed fur seal rookery
bears the name of Gavriil Pribilov, navigator for a Russian fur
company, who discovered the remote group. He named the first
island in June 1786 for his ship, the *Saint George*; the other large
island was named a year later to honor Saints Peter and Paul;
and the two smaller islands of the group, which comprise the

seal preserve, were subsequently given the faunal names, Otter and Walrus. [*See* Saint George Island; Saint Paul Island.]

Prince George (BC). Founded in 1807 as Fort George by Simon Fraser of the North West Company. With the coming of the Grand Trunk Pacific Railway, the railroad dubbed its "station town" Prince George, a name adopted by the electorate in 1915.

Prince of Wales Island (SEA). Largest of a cluster of islands in the Alexander Archipelago was named in 1793 by Capt. George Vancouver, RN, for the eldest son of his sovereign, George III. Infamous for his debauchery, Prince George Augustus Frederick was regent of England during his father's final attack of insanity, 1811–20, and reigned as George IV, 1820–30. [*See* Wales.]

Prince Rupert (BC). The Canadian marine gateway to Alaska, this town was named in 1906 as the result of a $250-contest for an appropriate title for the western terminus of the Grand Trunk Pacific Railway. The name honors the soldier-explorer cousin of King Charles II, who served as the first governor of "The Company of Adventurers of England Trading into Hudson's Bay," chartered by the king on 2 May 1670. [*See* Kelsey Bay.]

Prince William Sound (SCA). Named by Capt. George Vancouver, RN, in 1778 in honor of his monarch's third son, the eventual William IV of England. [*See* Clarence Strait.]

Prudhoe Bay, PRUHD-hoh (AA). Named by Sir John Franklin in 1826 to honor a fellow naval officer and African explorer, Algernon Percy, 4th duke of Northumberland and 1st Baron Prudhoe. Since oil exploration began in the North Slope region, there has been a tendency to corrupt the original English and long-standing Alaskan pronunciation to PROO-doh. [*See* Duke Island.]

Ptarmigan, TAR-muh-gan (SCA). Originating as a roadhouse in the Chugach Mountains on the old winter trail to Valdez, this area is now known primarily as Ptarmigan Drop for a sharp decline on the Richardson Highway. It is among three dozen creeks, gulches, lakes, and other assorted geographical features carrying the name of one of three species of grouse native to

Alaska. The willow ptarmigan (*Lagopus lagopus*), a feather-footed grouse which is white-plumed in winter, is the official bird of the state.

Puget Cape, PYOO-juht (SCA). Point of land between Port Bainbridge and Puget Bay on the southeast coast of the Kenai Peninsula was named in 1794 by Master Joseph Whidbey, RN, to honor Lt. Peter Puget, a superior officer in the British exploration expedition commanded by Capt. George Vancouver. A glacier, bay, and cove on the Kenai Peninsula and the peninsula between Yakutat Bay and Russell Fiord in Southeastern Alaska (in addition to Puget Sound in Washington State) also honor the same officer.

Pyramid Island (SEA). This island in Chilkat Inlet at the end of Lynn Canal bears a name descriptive of its appearance.

Q

Quartz Gulch (SEA). Named by Richard Harris, whose discovery of gold with Joseph Juneau in the Silver Bow Basin launched the gold rush of 1880. The gulch combines with 3 ravines and 33 streams in Alaska to pay tribute, via their names, to the gold-bearing mineral. [*See* Juneau.]

Queen Charlotte Islands (BC). Island group was named in July 1787 by Capt. George Dixon of the King George's Sound Company for his fur trading brig, *Queen Charlotte,* which in turn was named for the wife of King George III. [*See* Dixon Entrance.]

Queen Inlet (SEA). Name commemorates the S.S. *Queen,* first ship to navigate the upper reaches of Glacier Bay during the explorations of Muir Glacier in 1890–92 by Prof. Harry Fielding Reid. [See Glacier Bay; Reid Glacier.]

Queen Mary, Mount (YT). Peak in the Saint Elias range honors the wife of King George V, English monarch from 1910 to 1936. The queen, a cousin of the king, was the daughter of the duke of Teck of Germany.

Quincy Adams, Mount (SEA). The 3,560-foot peak straddling the U.S.-Canadian border in Glacier Bay National Monument was named in 1923 to honor the sixth president of the United States. As secretary of state in 1825, Adams negotiated the treaty with Russia that subsequently served as a guideline for the present boundary on which the mountain stands.

Quinhagak, KWIN-huh-gak (WA). Name of the Eskimo village on Kuskokwim Bay was spelled "Koingak" by the Russians in the 1820s and by the U.S. Census Bureau in 1970 as "Kwin-hagak," despite the present official spelling given in 1957 by the U.S. Board on Geographic Names. Regardless of the spelling differences, the name is said to mean "newly formed river" in reference to the constantly shifting delta channels of the Kusko-kwim River.

Quintino Sella Glacier, kwin-TEE-noh SEL-luh (SEA). Name assigned to honor a pioneer Italian Alpinist in 1897 by the first man to ascend Mount Saint Elias, Italian naval officer and explorer Luigi Amedeo Giuseppe Maria Ferdinando Francesco, the duke of the Abruzzi and prince of Savoy-Aosta.

R

Rampart (IA). Established during the Minook Creek gold strike of 1896, the village was first called Rampart City for the nearby rampartlike canyon of the Yukon River. Once comprising a population of 1,500, the town provided the setting for *The Barrier* by onetime resident, Rex Beach. The "mayor" of Rampart and grubstaker of the Russian-Indian miner, Minook, was Al Mayo, trading partner of Leroy Napoleon (Jack) McQuesten, the founder of Circle. [*See* Mayo.]

Rancheria, RANCH-er-EE-uh (YT). This settlement (Milepost 710) on the Alaska Highway takes its name from the paralleling river. First mentioned in an 1887 report by Canadian government geologist and surveyor George M. Dawson, the river was named in the late 1870s by American prospectors, ex-Californians who applied the Mexican term *rancheria,* meaning "farm compound," to an Indian settlement on the riverbank. [*See* Dawson Creek.]

Raspberry Island (SWA). A translation of the Russians' floral name for the island.

Rat Islands (SWA). Translation of the Russian name, Ostrova Krysii, which in turn was inspired by the Aleut name, *ayugadak* or "rat," for one island in the group. [*See* Aleutian Islands.]

Ray Mountains (IA). Name derives from that of the river by which Lt. Henry Tureman Allen, USA, aide to Gen. Nelson A. Miles, in 1885 honored another of the Alaskan commandant's noteworthy officers, Capt. Patrick Henry Ray. Captain Ray had established a meteorological station at Point Barrow in 1881. [*See* Allen Glacier.]

Red Devil (WA). This community derives its name from its major industry—the Red Devil Mercury Mine.

Reid Glacier (SEA). Named by the Harriman expedition of 1899 to honor geology professor Harry Fielding Reid of the Case School of Applied Sciences and Johns Hopkins University, who visited the Glacier Bay area in the early 1890s. [*See* Queen Inlet.]

Renard Island, ruh-NARD (SCA). Island in Resurrection Bay was arbitrarily given this French name by the USC&GS in 1905 as its English equivalent, "fox," had been frequently applied throughout Alaska. [*See* Fox Islands.]

Resurrection Bay (SCA). This name, duplicated in various geographic features on the Kenai Peninsula, is a translation of the Russian term for the bay, which meant "Resurrection Sunday harbor."

Revillagigedo Island, RUH-vee-uh-guh-GAY-doh (SEA). This Alexander Archipelago island, separated from the mainland by Behm Canal, was named in 1793 by Capt. George Vancouver, RN, in support of the name assigned the adjoining channel in the previous year by Spanish explorer Lt. Jacinto Caamaño. Caamaño was honoring Juan Vicente de Güemes Pacheco de Padilla Horcasitas y Aguayo, conde de Revilla Gigedo, who was viceroy of Mexico, 1789–94, during the controversy between England and Spain over claims (by right of first exploration) to the area surrounding Vancouver Island. While the Anglicized version of the island name, phonetically shown above, is simpler than the correct Spanish pronunciation, Alaskans generally shorten the title in conversation to "ruh-VIL-luh." [*See* Suemez Island.]

Rhino Peak (SEA). Also known as "Rhino Horn," the peak at the head of Mendenhall Glacier was named to describe its unique faunal conformation.

Richardson Highway. *See* Fort Richardson.

Richardson Mountains (YT). Name honors Sir John Richardson, surgeon and naturalist on the Franklin exploration expeditions of 1819–22 and 1825–27. Richardson also headed one of the early rescue parties that searched for the lost Franklin expedition of 1845–47. [*See* British Mountains.]

Robinson Mountains (SEA). The range between Bering and Guyot glaciers was named to honor Lt. L. I. Robinson, USRCS, who drowned while landing at Icy Bay in 1891.

Rocker Gulch (WA). This name, frequently assigned by miners, refers to a cradlelike device used to wash gold from sand and gravel in greater quantity than is possible with a gold pan. [*See* Goldpan Gulch; Placer Creek; Sluicebox Creek.]

Romanzof Mountains, roh-MAN-zawf (AA). Named in 1826

by Sir John Franklin to honor Count Nikolai Rumiantsev, one-time Russian chancellor who was a noted patron of scientific exploration. [*See* Cape Romanzof.]

Root, Mount (SEA). Peak straddling the Alaska-Canada border in the Saint Elias Mountains was named in 1908 by the USC&GS to honor Elihu Root, a member of the Alaska Boundary Tribunal of 1903. Root was U.S. secretary of war, 1899–1904; secretary of state, 1905–9; and U.S. senator from New York, 1909–15. [*See* Alverstone, Mount.]

Rootok Island, ROO-t<u>oo</u>k (SWA). The name assigned by the Russians to the Krenitzin group island is an example of the evolution of a word from its original language to its present form. The Aleut word *aikhak,* meaning "to travel," was adopted by the Russians and progressively altered to Aiktak, Aektok, and Ouektok until 1888, when a United States governmental agency converted it to its present form. [*See* Avatanak Island.]

Ross River (YT). Community name duplicates that of the river named by Hudson's Bay Company explorer-trader Robert Campbell in 1843 to honor Chief Factor Donald Ross.

Ruby (IA). Once a boom town of more than 1,000 residents, the community takes its name from nearby Ruby Creek, site of a gold strike in 1907. Other gold camps that sprang into being in the region included Long, Poorman, and Cripple.

Russell, Mount (IA). An 11,500-foot peak—the fourth highest within Mount McKinley National Park—a glacier in the Wrangell Mountains, an island in Glacier Bay National Monument, and a fiord in Yakutat Bay all honor Israel Cook Russell, USGS geologist, who explored Alaska with the USC&GS boundary expedition of 1889 and the National Geographic Society expedition of 1890.

Russian Mission (WA). Established in 1837 as the Russian-American Company's first fur trading post on the Yukon River, this community derives its name from the fact that it was also the site of the first Russian Orthodox church on the Yukon. The mission was built in 1851 by Creole (Russian-Aleut) priest Jacob Netzvetov.

Russian River (SEA). One of many geographic features reflecting early Russian ownership, exploration, and exploitation of the forty-ninth state. The river was the location of the first "official" discovery of gold in Alaska, when in 1850 Russian-Indian Creoles working under the direction of mining engineer Peter Doroshin sluiced gold from the stream. In the same era Doroshin founded a coal-mining operation at Port Graham; but in both instances the Russian-American Company withdrew its support, and the mineral potential of the region was allowed to remain dormant.

S

Sagavanirtok River, SAG-guh-vuh-NIRK-tuhk (AA). This North Slope river that heads between the Endicott and Philip Smith mountains and flows north 180 miles to empty into the Beaufort Sea east of Prudhoe Bay bears an Eskimo name meaning "strong current." Because of the length of its name, Alaskans generally refer to it as the "Sag."

Saint Cyr Range (YT). Name honors A. Saint-Cyr, who surveyed the Nisutlin River in 1898.

Saint Elias, Mount, uh-LEYE-uhs (YT). "First in Alaska, second in Canada, and third on the North American continent" is a capsule historic and geographic description of the 18,008-foot-high mountain that straddles the Alaska-Canada boundary. It is "first" because its sighting and purported naming by Russian explorer Vitus Bering, IRN, on Saint Elias' Day in 1741 is acknowledged as the official discovery of the Alaska mainland. It is second in height to Canada's highest mountain (Mount Logan, which is also in the Saint Elias range), and it ranks third after twin-peaked Mount McKinley and Mount Logan in the listing of the continent's tallest mountains. It is also the most westerly point in Canada, approximately 5,780 miles from the country's eastern extremity at Cape Spear, Newfoundland. [*See* Kayak Island.]

Saint Elias Mountains (SEA). The 90-mile-wide, 300-mile-long mountain range that forms the northern portion of the Canada–Alaska Panhandle boundary takes its name from its second highest peak, which was sighted and named by Vitus Bering, IRN, on Saint Elias' Day, 1741. Actually situated in Alaska, Yukon Territory, and British Columbia, the range contains several of the North American continent's highest mountains: the Yukon Territory's Mount Logan (19,850 feet), the highest peak in Canada and second highest mountain in North America (after Alaska's twin-peaked Mount McKinley); Mount Saint Elias, straddling the Alaska–Yukon Territory border, the third highest mountain on the continent at 18,008 feet; and 15,300-foot Mount Fairweather, astride the Alaska–British Columbia border, the highest point in the province. [*See* Alaska Range.]

Saint George Island (WA). The island was named by its discoverer, Gavriil Pribilov, in June 1776 for his ship, the *Saint George*. [*See* Pribilof Islands.]

Saint Lawrence Island (WA). Discovered and named by Vitus Bering, IRN, on 10 August 1728—Saint Lawrence's Day—while on a voyage commissioned by Russian Tsar Peter the Great to determine if Asia and America were joined or separate entities.

Saint Michael (WA). Community on the tundra island of the same name in southeastern Norton Sound was established about 1833 as a fortified post, Mikhailovskii Redut, named after the name saint of Capt. Mikhail Dmitrievich Tebenkov, IRN, who charted the area in 1831 and subsequently served as governor of Russian America. The name was soon changed to Fort Saint Michael and the town served as the starting point for Russian excursions to the interior. After American purchase, Saint Michael became the deepwater port where ocean-going vessels transferred cargo to shallow-draft stern-wheelers for cartage up the Yukon River. The first gold from the Klondike passed through Saint Michael en route to Seattle, and the town boomed as the jumping-off point for gold seekers journeying upriver to the Dawson diggings.

Saint Paul Island (WA). Largest of the Pribilof Islands was originally called Saint Peter and Saint Paul, as it was first sighted on 12 June 1787—the day dedicated jointly on the Julian Calendar to those two apostles—by fur hunters on Saint George Island 30 miles away. In time the dual name gave way to the present short form. [*See* Pribilof Islands.]

Salmon River (IA). Name of this stream rising in the Baird Mountains is a translation of the descriptive Eskimo title, Kallagunick. The word "salmon" is common as both a faunal and floral name in Alaska, as in Salmon Bay or Salmonberry Cove, for example.

Salt Chuck (SEA). The name is a Chinook Jargon term meaning "salt water" and is descriptive of the village's location on Kasaan Bay.

Sanak Islands, suh-NAK (SWA). Name for the group of rocks and two islands—Sanak and Caton—southeast of Unimak Island is derived from an Aleut term, *sannakh,* of unknown meaning.

San Clemente Island (SEA). This Alexander Archipelago island was named by Capt. Juan Francisco de la Bodega y Quadra and his navigator, Francisco Antonio Maurelle, in 1779 to honor Saint Clement. [*See* Portillo Channel.]

Sand Point (SWA). This Popof Island community's name is adopted from the adjacent low, flat, sandy spit descriptively called "Sand Point" in 1872 by William Healey Dall, USC&GS.

San Fernando Island (SEA). This island in the western sector of the Alexander Archipelago was named in May 1779 by Francisco Antonio Maurelle, pilot and second in command to Capt.

Juan Francisco de la Bodega y Quadra during their second voyage to Alaska waters. The island was visited twice, on 21 May and 30 May, and was presumably named on the second visit, San Fernando's Day, in honor of King Ferdinand III of Spain (canonized by Pope Clement X).

Sanford, Mount (IA). Located in the Wrangell Mountains, this 16,237-foot mountain was named by Lt. Henry Tureman Allen, USA, for his great-grandfather, Reuben Sanford. [*See* Allen Glacier.]

Sargent Icefield (SCA). Name honors USGS topographer Rufus Harvey Sargent, who mapped the Kenai Peninsula.

Savoonga, suh-VOONG-guh (WA). This Saint Lawrence Island community bears an Eskimo name of unrecorded meaning.

Saxman (SEA). A suburb of Ketchikan, this community was founded as a Tlingit Indian village in 1894. Its name honors the memory of Samuel Saxman, a schoolteacher at Tongass Village and Loring, who drowned in 1886 while in search of a site for a new, united village.

Scammon Bay (WA). The village is named for the nearby bay, which honors Capt. Charles M. Scammon, USRCS, who served as marine chief of the Western Union Telegraph Expedition of 1865–67.

Schwatka Mountains (AA). Named by Lt. George M. Stoney, USN, to honor Lt. Frederick Schwatka, USA, explorer-writer who led a search expedition for the lost Franklin party in 1879–80, rafted the Yukon River from source to mouth in 1883, and participated in a New York *Herald* expedition that mapped the Mount Saint Elias area in 1886. A peak northeast of Livengood also bears his name, an easier to pronounce but less descriptive USA substitution in 1902 for the Indian name, Mkleetokumenah, meaning "mountain with lake on top."

Sealers Island (SEA). Island in Muir Inlet of Glacier Bay National Monument was so named because it was a seal hunting ground for local Indians. The historic importance of the seal to the Alaska natives—Aleuts, Eskimos, and Indians—and to fur-hunting white men is evidenced by the application of this faunal name, or variations of it, to over 50 geographic features throughout Alaska waters. Now protected by law, the once-endangered fur seal was wantonly slaughtered by man: for instance, 240,000 were killed in the Seal Islands group in 1868. [*See* Pribilof Islands.]

Sea Lion Rock (WA). The name of this rock in the Pribilof Islands is a translation of the Russian title, Kamen' Sivuchii, which reflected the rock's use as a rookery for the large, eared member of the seal family. Several geographic features in Alaska waters bear this faunal name, and one species of sea lion is named after Georg Steller, German-born naturalist on the Bering expedition of 1741. [*See* Steller, Mount.]

Seattle, Mount (SEA). This 10,070-foot mountain in the Saint Elias range was named by Israel Cook Russell, USGS, in 1890 to honor the city of Seattle, which, in turn, was named for Chief Sealth of the Duwamish and Suquamish tribes of Puget Sound in Washington State. [*See* Russell, Mount.]

Seduction Point (SEA). Southern tip of Chilkat Peninsula was so named by Capt. George Vancouver, RN, because of the "designing nature" of the Indians whom Master Joseph Whidbey encountered there.

Seguam Island, SE-gwuhm (SWA). This Andreanof island and nearby Seguam Pass were initially named Ostrov Segouam and Sigouam Détroit, respectively. The common element in their names derived from an Aleut word pertaining to "bird colony."

Selawik, SEL-luh-wik (AA). Eskimo village takes its name from the nearby lake bearing a native name for a species of fish.

Seldovia, sel-DOH-vee-uh (SCA). This community situated on the southwest coast of the Kenai Peninsula derives its name from the Russian Zaliv Sel'devoi, meaning "herring bay." [*See* Kachemak Bay.]

Selkirk. *See* Fort Selkirk.

Selwyn Mountains (YT). Name honors Dr. A. R. C. Selwyn, a director of the Canadian Geological Survey.

Semichi Islands, se-MEE-chee (SWA). Name derives from *semik*, a Russian religious day—the seventh Thursday after Easter—on which Vitus Bering, RN, discovered the small chain of islands, which belong to the Near group.

Semidi Islands, se-MEE-dee (SWA). The original Russian name, Ostrova Semidi, approximately translates as "seven islands."

Semisopochnoi Island, sem-suh-PAWSH-noi (SWA). The third largest member of the Rat Islands bears a Russian name meaning "seven peaks," coined from the words *sem,* or "seven," and *sopochka,* meaning "dormant volcano." It is the first point in the Aleutian Archipelago to be technically in the Eastern Hemisphere and, hence, is the easternmost point in the USA. [*See* Amatignak Island; Barrow.]

Seniavin, Cape, sen-YAH-vuhn (SWA). Named by Capt. Feodor Petrovich Lütke, IRN, for his ship, *Seniavin.* Lütke, whose name is commemorated by a cape on Unimak Island, commanded a two-ship exploration of the Bering Sea, 1828, and named many features on the north coast of the Alaska Peninsula. [*See* Moller, Port.]

Seversens, SEE-ver-suhnz (SCA). Situated on Roadhouse Bay on the north shore of Iliamna Lake, both the site and bay derive their names from Severn's Roadhouse.

Seward, SOO-erd (SCA). This Kenai Peninsula city was founded in 1902 by surveyors for the Alaska Railroad and named for Secretary of State William H. Seward, who had spearheaded the move to purchase Alaska from Russia in 1867. The name was suggested by Prof. Edmond S. Meany of the University of Washington. Alternate proposals include Almouth, for "mouth of Alaska," and Vituska, to honor Vitus Bering. A peninsula that juts 200 miles into the Bering Sea between Norton and Kotzebue sounds is also named for Secretary Seward. It was variously called Kaviak,

Sumner, or Nome Peninsula prior to 1900. When Rev. John Green Brady, a former Presbyterian missionary, was appointed as the fifth governor of the territory, he officially suggested adoption of the new name, and during his tenure in office, 1897–1906, the old names were dropped and the present title appeared on maps.

Seymour Canal (SEA). This Admiralty Island inlet was explored by Master Joseph Whidbey, RN, in 1794, and named by his commander, Capt. George Vancouver, to honor a British peer, Sir Hugh Seymour. The estuary and its small islands comprise a bald eagle nesting area, the most densely populated in North America. They are located at the center of a total of 10,788 acres in the Tongass National Forest designated as a management preserve for the endangered species. [*See* Tongass National Forest.]

Shageluk, SHAG-uh-luhk (WA). An Ingalik Indian name meaning "village of the dog people."

Shaman Island, SHAY-muhn (SEA). Small island in Stephens Passage off the west coast of Douglas Island bears an Indian name meaning "medicine man."

Sheep Mountain (YT). Peak near the head of Kluane Lake is one of a multitude of geographic features throughout the Northland to which early trappers and prospectors indiscriminately affixed the term "sheep," a nickname for the several species of wild mountain sheep and goats indigenous to the region.

Sheldon Point (WA). Village takes its name from the nearby point at the south mouth of the Yukon River, which bears the surname of the operator of a saltery at the site.

Shelikof Strait, SHEL-luh-kawf (SWA). Named for Russian fur trader Grigorii Ivanovich Shelikhov who, with his partner Ivan Golikov, founded the first permanent white settlement in Alaska in 1783. The Shelikhov Company established a series of trading posts along the Alaska coast and eventually became the powerful Russian-American Company headed by Alexander Baranov. [*See* Kodiak Island.]

Shemya Island, SHEM-yuh (SWA). Site of Shemya AFS, the most westerly of all U.S. "Stateside" military installations. The name of this Semichi island is of unverified origin.

Shishaldin Volcano, shi-SHAWL-duhn (SWA). Russianized spelling of the native name for the 6,600-foot-high volcanic peak on Unimak Island.

Shishmaref, SHISH-mah-ref (AA). Community name derives from that of the adjacent inlet, which was named in 1816 by Lt. Otto von Kotzebue, IRN, to honor his second in command, Lt. Gleb Shishmarev. [*See* Cape Romanzof; Kotzebue.]

Shublik Mountains (AA). Name is a translation of an Eskimo word meaning "spring."

Shumagin Islands, SHOO-muh-gin (SWA). Islands off the southern tip of the Alaska Peninsula were named by Vitus Bering, IRN, after one of the *Saint Peter*'s seamen who died of scurvy and was buried on one of the small islands of the group—possibly Nagai Island—on 30 August 1741.

Shungnak Village, SHUNG-nak (AA). Eskimo community on the Kobuk River takes its name from a nearby tributary stream whose native name means "jade," as the gem stone is found at its headwaters in the Schwatka Mountains.

Sikanni Chief River, si-KAN-ee (BC). Title honors the local Indians, whose tribal name means "people of the big rocks [or mountains]."

Silver Bow Basin (SEA). Named for the Silver Bow Mine in Montana by Richard Harris who, with his partner Joseph Juneau, made the gold strike in this basin that created the city of Juneau in 1880. [*See* Juneau.]

Silver City (YT). Early prospectors' name for the boom town on the southeast shore of the Yukon Territory's largest lake, now the ghost town of Kluane. [*See* Kluane Lake.]

Simeonof Island, SEYE-muh-nawf (SWA). Name of this Shumagin island is a Russian variation of the name Simon.

Simpson, Cape (AA). The name of this point of land on the

Beaufort Sea honors George Simpson, governor of the Hudson's Bay Company. It was named on 28 July 1837 by Thomas Simpson and Peter Warren Dease, leaders of a Hudson's Bay Company exploration expedition that traversed the Arctic coast from the mouth of the Mackenzie River to Point Barrow. Two other geographic features on the Beaufort Sea named Simpson—a lagoon and a cove—honor Thomas Simpson. [*See* Dease River; Franklin Mountains.]

Simpson Range (YT). Mountains honor Sir George Simpson, first governor of Hudson's Bay Company following its amalgamation with the North West Company. [*See* Frances Lake.]

Sitka, SIT-kuh (SEA). Administrative capital of Russian America, 1804–67, and of Alaska Territory, 1867–1906, the city derives its name from the Tlingit word *shitka,* meaning "by the sea," which was the native term for the whole of Baranof Island. Following destruction of Old Sitka, or Mikhailovskii Redut (Fort Saint Michael), which was built in 1799 and razed by Tlingit warriors in 1802, Alexander Andreevich Baranov returned to the island, defeated the natives, and constructed Novoarkhangelsk. This fortified town became headquarters for the Russian-American Company and the seat of government for Russian America, a territory stretching along the Pacific Coast from the Arctic to Fort Ross, California. With the purchase of Alaska by the United States in 1867, the city adopted its present name. Sitka National Monument, established on 23 March 1910, marks the site of the Indian "fortified" log town destroyed by Russian and Aleut forces, which were led by Governor Baranov and supported by the cannons of the *Neva,* commanded by Capt. Yurii Federovich Lisianskii, IRN, when Sitka was recaptured from the Tlingits in 1804. [*See* Baranof Island.]

Sitkinak Islands, SIT-kuh-nak (SWA). Part of the Trinity group, these islands bear a Russian adaptation of an Aleut word, meaning unknown.

Sixtymile River (YT). So named because it enters the Yukon

River approximately 60 miles upstream from old Fort Reliance. [*See* Fort Reliance; Fortymile River; Twelvemile Creek.]

Skagway (SEA). While popularly believed to be a translation of a climatically appropriate Indian word, *skagua,* meaning "home of the north wind," the name more logically derives from the Tlingit term, *sch-kawai,* which means "end of the salt water" and describes the site's position near the end of Lynn Canal's Taiya Inlet. Initially settled in 1888 by 74-year-old ex-steamboat captain William Moore, the town briefly became a city of 15,000 people while serving as the "Gateway to the Yukon" during the gold rush. It was the starting point for the trail over White Pass to Lake Bennett and the Yukon River headwaters, and in 1900 became the southern terminus of the 110-mile-long White Pass and Yukon Railroad to Whitehorse. [*See* Dyea; White Pass.]

Skeena River (BC). The name is of Indian derivation and means "water that comes out of the clouds."

Skukum, Mount (YT). Peak west of Carcross bears a variation of the Chinook Jargon word *skookum,* meaning "big" or "strong."

Skwentna (SCA). Name reflects the settlement's location near the junction of the Skwentna and Yentna rivers. The Indian suffix *na* means "river," but the roots *skwent* and *yent* are of undetermined definition.

Slana (IA). Indian village and adjacent river have an Indian name of unknown definition.

Sleetmute (IA). The USCG in 1913 reported that this village bore a phonetic adaptation of an Eskimo term *sleitmut,* meaning "whetstone people."

Sluicebox Creek (IA). A name assigned by miners refers to a ribbed-bottom trough through which gold-bearing material is washed so that the flowing water carries away the gravel and leaves the heavier gold caught in the riffles or cleats. [*See* Goldpan Gulch; Placer Creek; Rocker Gulch.]

Smithers (BC). Name honors Sir Alfred W. Smithers, a director of the Grand Trunk Pacific Railway.

Soldiers Summit (YT). Milepost 1061 on the Alaska Highway marks the location of the formal opening of the old Alcan Highway on 20 November 1942. It was so named in honor of the military men who constructed the roadway. [*See* Alcan Highway.]

Soldotna, sohl-DAHT-nuh (SCA). The town that developed in the late 1930s around the junction of the Kenai Road with the Sterling Highway adopted its name from Soldotna Creek. The origin of the stream's name, which appeared as "Suldahtnah" on 1918 USCS maps, has been explained in three different ways. The most accepted version traces the name from the Russian word soldat or "soldier." Another theory is that its 1918 name spelling was an Indian word for "stream fork." The third hypothesis contends it is an adaptation of tseldatna, a type of Indian herb growing in the locale.

Sourdough Gulch (IA). Name applied to a ravine is the Alaska-Yukon miners' slang term for a person who has wintered in the Northland. It comes from the prospectors' and trappers' custom of carrying a starter of fermented dough to make sourdough pan bread. [*See* Cheechako Gulch.]

Sparrevohn Air Force Station, SPAIR-uh-vawn (IA). Situated midway between Anchorage and Kuskokwim Bay, this military installation is named for Capt. Frank Sparrevohn, USAF helicopter pilot, who selected the radar station site in 1951.

Spenard, spuh-NAHRD (SCA). The city, a suburb of Anchorage, was named for early settler Joseph A. Spenard, who homesteaded on the shore of Lake Spenard, which is now home port for one of the world's largest flotillas of float planes.

Spencer, Cape (SEA). Named by Capt. George Vancouver, RN, in 1794 to honor George John Spencer, the Viscount Althorp and 2nd earl of Spencer, who was first lord of the Admiralty, 1794–1801. A distant forebear of Sir Winston Leonard Spencer Churchill, England's prime minister during World War II, the earl had an illustrious career that included suppression of the Royal

Navy mutinies at Spithead and The Nore in the late 1790s and the distinction of having picked Lord Horatio Nelson as fleet commander in the Mediterranean.

Spencer, Point (AA). Named in 1827 by Capt. Frederick W. Beechey, RN, to honor a fellow officer.

Spuhn Island (SEA). This small island at the west entrance of Gastineau Channel was named in 1880 by Comdr. Lester A. Beardslee, USN, of the U.S.S. *Jamestown,* which policed and examined Alaska waters. The name honors German-born Carl Spuhn of the Northwest Trading Company who managed the company store in Juneau.

Squanga Lake (YT). An Indian name meaning "round fish."

Squaw Rapids (YT). Name of the dangerous rapids in the Yukon River immediately below Miles Canyon is one example of the frequent geographic use in the Northland of the term generally used to mean an Indian woman. Another Squaw Rapids, at the juncture of the Koyukuk and Glacier rivers in Alaska, was so named when an Indian woman drowned in the broiling water. The word was adopted by the white man from the Algonquin-speaking tribes of the East Coast of North America whose *eshqua* meant "female deer."

Starrigavan Bay, STAHR-gav-uhn (SEA). Russian term meaning "old harbor" was applied to the bay on the west coast of Baranof Island because it was the site of the first Russian fur trading post in the area. Established by Alexander Andreevich Baranov in 1799, it was destroyed by Tlingit Indians in 1802. [*See* Sitka.]

Stebbins (WA). The name of this community on Saint Michael Island was changed from the Eskimo name of Atroik to Stebbins in the latter part of the nineteenth century as a geographic tie-in to its location on the shore of Stephens Pass. The present spelling is a phonetic substitution of "b" for the sounds of "f," "ph," and "v" in the speech patterns of early-day bilingual Eskimos.

Steese Highway, STEES (IA). Known as the "Road to the Midnight Sun," the highway connecting Fairbanks and Circle was named for Gen. James G. Steese, USA, a former president of the Alaska Road Commission. [*See* Eagle Summit.]

Steller, Mount (SWA). A cove on Attu Island and two identically named mountains—a 7,300-foot peak in the Katmai National Monument and a 10,267-foot glaciered peak in the Chugach range—honor Georg Steller, German-born naturalist on the Bering expedition of 1741. Steller went ashore on Kayak Island for scientific observations and confirmed discovery of the Alaska mainland by identifying a crested jay native only to the North American continent. [*See* Saint Elias Mountains.]

Stephens Passage (SEA). Named in 1794 by Capt. George Vancouver, RN, to honor Sir Philip Stephens, secretary to the British Admiralty, 1763–95.

Sterling (SCA). A community and the Sterling Highway (Alaska Route 1) were named in honor of Hawley Sterling, engineer for the Alaska Road Commission.

Stevens Village (IA). Village originally bore the Indian name Denyeet, meaning "canyon," but was renamed in 1902 to honor the election of one of its founders, Old Steven, as chief.

Stewart (BC). Community at the head of Portland Canal was named for miners Robert and John Stewart who founded the settlement in the early 1900s. [*See* Portland Canal.]

Stewart River (YT). Community name duplicates that of the river named by Hudson's Bay Company explorer-trader Robert Campbell to honor his assistant, James G. Stewart.

Stikine River, sti-KEEN (SEA). Heading in British Columbia and flowing across the Alaska-Canada border into Eastern Passage north of Wrangell, this 335-mile-long river bears a Tlingit Indian name meaning "great river."

Stony River (IA). This Indian village derives its name from the descriptive title given the adjacent stream by prospectors ca. 1900.

Stuart Island (SWA). This Norton Sound island was named in

1778 by Capt. James Cook, RN, presumably for John Stuart, 3rd earl of Bute, prime minister of England, 1762–63, and supporter of arts and sciences in later years.

Suckling, Cape (SCA). Named by Capt. James Cook, RN, in 1778 to honor Maurice Suckling, the comptroller of the Royal Navy at the time of Cook's third voyage and an uncle of England's most famous naval hero, Lord Horatio Nelson. [*See* Controller Bay.]

Suemez Island, SWAY-muhs (SEA). Initially this Alexander Archipelago island was given the Spanish name Isla Suemez in the late 1770s by Capt. Juan Francisco de la Bodega y Quadra. It was subsequently charted as Güemes by Capt. Dionisio Alcalá Galiano in 1792. The meaning of the original (and official) name is unknown, but the alternate title was an obvious attempt to solve the mystery by "correcting" the spelling to honor Juan Vicente de Güemes Pacheco de Padilla Horcasitas y Aguayo, conde de Revilla Gigedo, the viceroy of Mexico from 1789 to 1794. [*See* Bucareli Bay; Revillagigedo Island.]

Sukkwan Island, suhk-WAHN (SEA). This 44,204-acre island in the Alexander Archipelago derives its name from a Tlingit Indian word *suq-qan,* meaning "grassy village."

Sumdum Glacier (SEA). A glacier, mountain, island, and former settlement bear a name of Tlingit Indian origin meaning "tranquil," referring to the absence of storms in the sheltered Holkham Bay area.

Summit (IA). Initially a railroad camp, this settlement is located at the summit of Broad Pass.

Sumner Strait (SEA). Waterway between Kupreanof and Prince of Wales islands in the Alexander Archipelago was named in 1875 by William Healey Dall of the USC&GS for Senator Charles Sumner of Massachusetts, who was a key figure in securing ratification of Secretary of State William Seward's purchase of Alaska. [*See* Alaska.]

Suntrana, suhn-TRAN-uh (IA). Purportedly an Indian name

meaning "burning hills," supposedly for ground steam during rainstorms.

Susitna, soo-SIT-nuh (IA). A river which the Indians called Sushitna, meaning "sandy river," has given its name to the glacier in the Alaska Range where it heads, and to a mountain and village near its mouth on Cook Inlet. The original spelling has been modified in the interest of propriety.

Sutton (SCA). Community on the Glenn Highway northeast of Palmer was established in 1918 as a station on the Alaska Railroad, but the railroad has no information pertaining to the name source.

Swift River (YT). Community name is that of the descriptive title for the adjacent river.

T

Tagish, TAG-ish (YT). Named for the Indian tribe, members of the Taku subdivision of Tlingit, who resided in the vicinity.

Taiya River (SEA). *See* Dyea.

Taku Inlet, TAH-koo (SEA). Used extensively for various geographic features in the Juneau area, Taku is the name of the subdivision of Tlingit Indians that inhabited the locale. The name is purportedly a contraction of the Tlingit Indian word *tak-wakh-tha-ku,* meaning "place where the geese sit down." Taku Arm and Taku River to the east in British Columbia have the same name source, while Taku Channel in the Bering Sea is the namesake of a USC&GS steamer, the *Taku.* The Canadian pronunciation of the name, TA-koo, differs from that employed by Alaskans.

Talkeetna, tawl-KEET-nuh (SCA). Once the site of a Tanaina

Indian village, this community is the outgrowth of a work camp established ca. 1916 during the construction of the Alaska Railroad. The name is a native term meaning "river of plenty."

Tanacross, TAN-uh-kraws (IA). Originally a telegraph station known as "Tanana [River] Crossing." The name was contracted to its present form in 1932 at the suggestion of the Bureau of Indian Affairs.

Tanadak Island, TAN-uh-dak (SWA). A Russian place name derived from the Aleut word *tanadakh,* meaning "burial [eternal] ground," has been applied to this island in the Delarof group.

Tanaga Island, TAN-uh-guh (SWA). The name of this Andreanof group island derives from an Aleut word that means "great [is]land itself."

Tanalian River, tuh-NAY-lee-uhn (SCA). Several features—a mountain, former village site, and a point of land on the shore of Lake Clark near Port Alsworth—derive their names from that of the lake's feeder stream, which the Tanaina Indians descriptively called "strong falls." [*See* Port Alsworth.]

Tanana, TAN-nuh-naw (IA). Name of the village at the junction of Yukon and Tanana rivers comes from the Indian name Tananah, meaning "river trail." The Tanana, formed by the Chisna and Nabesna rivers, is Alaska's largest tributary to the Yukon River.

Tangent Point (AA). Descriptive name given by Hudson's Bay Company explorer Thomas Simpson in 1837 because the land formed "an acute angle, well termed Point Tangent." [*See* Dease River; Harrison Bay.]

Tantallon Point, TANT-uhl-lawn (SEA). The name of this southeastern tip of Douglas Island and the name of nearby Marmion Island are examples of William Healey Dall's frequently used technique of linking neighboring geographic features with subtle, often humorous, historically related names. Tantallon was a castle in Sir Walter Scott's poem, "Marmion," which dealt with the Douglas clan of Scotland. [*See* Marmion Island.]

Tatalina Air Force Station, TAT-uh-LEE-nuh (IA). Interior Alaska has two Tatalina rivers—one north of McGrath, the other northwest of Fairbanks. The former is the site of the military installation. The Indian name is of unrecorded meaning.

Tatum, Mount, TAY-tum (IA). This 11,140-foot peak in Mount McKinley National Park was named for Robert G. Tatum, a postulant at the Indian mission at Nenana, who was a member of the first party officially to scale Mount McKinley's 20,320-foot South Peak, on 7 June 1913. [*See* McKinley, Mount.]

Taylor (BC). Center of a natural gas field from which gas is piped to the Washington-Oregon-California area, the town is named for Hudson's Bay Company employee David Taylor, who arrived in the locale around 1912.

Taylor Highway (IA). The name of the highway from Tetlin Junction to Eagle honors a former chief engineer of the Alaska Road Commission, Ike P. Taylor.

Taylor Mountains (IA). Named for a miner who prospected the region.

Tazimina Lakes, taz-uh-MEE-nuh (SCA). The lakes' name, deriving from that of the river that feeds and joins them, is a Tanaina Indian title stemming from the term for "trap."

Tazlina Lake, taz-LEE-nuh (SCA). Glacier, lake, and river derive their names from the Indian term *taslintna,* meaning "swift river."

Tee Harbor (SEA). Bay north of Juneau was so named because of its T-shaped appearance.

Telegraph Creek (BC). A trading post on the Stikine Trail during the gold rush to the Klondike, it got its name in 1866 as the site of a Stikine River crossing of the proposed Old World-to-New World telegraph line via Bering Strait. [*See* Burns Lake; Laberge, Lake.]

Teller (AA). Founded as a gold camp ca. 1900, the community adopted the name of nearby Teller Reindeer Station established by Sheldon Jackson in 1892 to train Eskimos in the herding of reindeer imported from Siberia. The name honors Henry M. Teller, Colorado's first senator, who served as secretary of the interior, 1882–85. [*See* Brevig Mission; Jackson Island.]

Terrace (BC). So named because of the terraced levels along the Skeena River near the townsite.

Teslin, TEZ-lin (YT). The community's name, adopted from that of the nearby lake, is an Indian word meaning "long waters." During the Klondike Gold Rush, the 86-mile-long waterway straddling the Yukon–British Columbia border was a way point on the Stikine Trail, which ran from Fort Wrangell up the Stikine River to Telegraph Creek, then 150 miles overland to Teslin Lake, and down the Teslin and Yukon rivers to Dawson. [*See* Nisutlin Bay.]

Tetlin (IA). Village, lake, river, and Alaska Highway junction derive their names from the Tetlin Indian Reservation, named for Chief Tetlin.

Thane (SEA). Suburb of Juneau was initially a prospectors' camp known as Sheep Creek. The name was changed in 1914 to honor Bartlett L. Thane, general manager of the Alaska Gastineau Mining Company situated at the townsite.

Theodore, Point (SEA). The southern tip of Yakobi Island in the northwest sector of the Alexander Archipelago is one of 8 geographic features in the locale to honor Capt. Yurii Federovich Lisianskii, IRN, an explorer who aided in re-establishing the Russians in Sitka following the Indian massacre of 1802. The name "Theodore" is an anglicized version of "Federovich." [*See* Lisianski Peninsula.]

Thetis Island, THEE-tis (AA). A name prevalent on geographic features of the Arctic Slope and repeated in the Alexander Archipelago is that of the revenue cutter *Thetis,* which patrolled Alaska waters in the 1880s.

Thorne Bay (SEA). Names of the community, river, lake, head, and bay on, in addition to a small island off the coast of, Prince of Wales Island are misspelled tributes to Franklin Thorn,

USC&GS superintendent, 1885–89. However, Thorne Arm on Revillagigedo Island is a correctly spelled USC&GS tribute to mariner Charles Thorne, captain of the steamer *California* which made the run between Portland, Oregon, and Southeastern Alaska ports carrying passengers, mail, and freight.

Three Saints Harbor (SWA). Historic harbor and Three Saints Bay derive their names from the *Three Saints,* a Shelikhov Company ship that carried Russian fur traders to the site in 1783. The company headquarters was the first permanent white settlement in Alaska. [*See* Kodiak Island.]

Tigalda Island, ti-GAHL-duh (SWA). An Aleut word of undeterminable meaning assigned by the Russians to this island in the Krenitzin group and variously spelled Coagalga, Kagalga, Kigalga, and Tigalga. [*See* Avatanak Island.]

Tin City (AA). This mining camp south of Cape Prince of Wales was so named because of tin ore discovered in the area in 1903. Although relatively dormant for several decades, the community has recently reactivated because of ore development currently underway in the immediate locale.

Tofty (IA). Former mining camp, virtually abandoned since the mid-1940s, was named for A. F. Tofty, who discovered gold in the area in 1908 and took out 376 ounces in six weeks.

Togiak, TOH-gee-yak (WA). One of two villages in the immediate area bearing an adaptation of the Eskimo name Togiagamute, meaning "Togiaga people." To differentiate between the two settlements, the southernmost was called "Owens" after trading post operator Johnny Owens.

Tok, TOHK (IA). Junction of the Glenn Highway with the Alaska Highway, the community developed since the 1940s and was the location of the U.S. Customs and Immigration office until the Port Alcan facility was established. The name was adopted from that of the Tok River, an Indian name of unverified meaning.

Toklat River (IA). This tributary of the Kantishna River bears an Indian name descriptive of its color, which was loosely translated to mean "dish water." [*See* Kantishna.]

Tongass National Forest, TAWNG-guhs (SEA). Created in 1907 by the presidential proclamation of Theodore Roosevelt, the United States' largest national forest bears a name of unverified derivation. It possibly comes from the name of a Tlingit Indian clan whose community house featured pillars carved with sea lion symbols and who referred to themselves as the *tangas nit quou* or "sea lion pillar people." The word *tahn* in the Tlingit tongue means sea lion and was the native name for Prince of Wales Island. [*See* Yakutat.]

Too Much Gold Creek (YT). Dawson area stream was so named in ironic jest because Robert Henderson, codiscoverer of the Klondike Strike, found it to be goldless. [*See* Carmacks; Gold Bottom Creek.]

Top of the World Highway (YT). The descriptive official name of the Yukon Territory's summertime Highway 10 that runs west from Dawson to the Alaska border.

Totem Bay, TOH-tem (SEA). This bay next to Kupreanof Island was so named by the USC&GS in 1886 because pillars of rock on its shore resembled the Indian totem poles prevalent throughout southeast Alaska. The term was loosely adopted by the white man from the Chippewa Indian word *ototeman*, meaning "brother-sister kin," and applied to the carved poles of Northwest Coast Indians—house poles and mortuary poles—decorated with heraldic clan or family crests and mythological symbols.

Tracy Arm (SEA). Waterway that merges with Endicott Arm and flows into Stephens Passage from the mainland is a glacier-headed fiord named in 1889 for Benjamin Franklin Tracy, an army general in the Civil War and secretary of the navy under President Benjamin Harrison. [*See* Endicott Mountains.]

Trident, Mount, TREYE-dent (SWA). Name, assigned by the National Geographic Society in 1916, is descriptive of the three peaks of this 6,790-foot volcano in Katmai National Monument.

Trinity Islands (SWA). The original English name was bestowed by Capt. James Cook, RN, in 1778 and subsequently confirmed on the charts of Spanish naval officers as Isla Trinidad and by the Russians as Ostrova Troitsy.

Trutch (BC). Named after English civil engineer Sir Joseph W. Trutch, the first lieutenant governor of British Columbia.

Tsirku Glacier, SIR-koo (SEA). Glacier and river bear a Tlingit Indian term meaning "big salmon," one of the alternate names of the stream.

Tugidak Island, TOO-guh-dak (SWA). Name of this island in the Trinity group was derived by the Russians from an Aleut word meaning "moon."

Tuluksak, tuh-LOOK-sak (WA). Eskimo village name means "raven."

Tundra Creek (AA). A descriptive and oft-repeated name derived from a Russian term meaning "mossy plain." The nearly level and treeless plains are found chiefly north of the Arctic Circle in the Northland and equivalent in many respects to a bog except for their underlayer of permafrost (a modern coined contraction of "permanent" and "frost"), which is a subsoil perennially frozen below a summer-thaw depth of six to eight inches. The tundra vegetation, particularly lichen, supports wild caribou and their imported cousins, the reindeer.

Tuntutuliak, TOON-tuh-TOO-lee-yak (WA). Eskimo village name means "many reindeer."

Turnagain Arm (SCA). Charted as River Turnagain in 1778 by Capt. James Cook, RN, when his ship was forced to turn back in its quest for a Pacific-Atlantic water route. In 1794 Capt. George Vancouver, RN, a former midshipman on the Cook voyage, more extensively explored the waterway and confirmed that it was not a major river; hence, he renamed Cook's River as Cook Inlet and River Turnagain as Turnagain Arm. [*See* Cook Inlet.]

Turner, Mount (SEA). Peak straddling the Alaska-Canada border in the Saint Elias Mountains was named in 1908 by the USC&GS

to honor George Turner, a member of the Alaska Boundary Tribunal of 1903 and a former U.S. senator from Washington State. [*See* Alverstone, Mount.]

Twelvemile Creek (YT). So named because it joins the Yukon River 12 miles downstream from old Fort Reliance. [*See* Fort Reliance; Fortymile River; Sixtymile River.]

Tyee, TEYE-ee (SEA). Settlement on Admiralty Island and other geographic features in southeast Alaska bear a native word meaning "anyone of superior status" or, literally, "chief."

Tyndall Glacier (SEA). Glacier at the head of Icy Bay was named by the 1886 *New York Times* Expedition for nineteenth-century British physicist and glacial expert John Tyndall.

Tyonek, teye-OH-nik (SCA) Initially a Tanaina Indian village listed in the 1880 census as having a population of 2 whites, 6 creoles, and 109 natives, the community got its name from the Indian word meaning "little chief."

U

Ugamak Island, OO-guh-mak (SWA). An Aleut word meaning "ceremony" has been affixed to this Krenitzin group island.

Ukivok, OO-kee-vuhk (AA). Village bears the original Eskimo name for King Island on which it is located. Early-day natives lived in rock dwellings that were, in effect, enlargements of fissures in the island's cliffs.

Ukolnoi Island, oo-KOHL-noi (SWA). Name for this Pavlof island is an adaptation of the original Russian name, Ostrov Yukol'noi or Ugol'noi, meaning "stone coal."

Ulak Island, OO-lak (SWA). Island in the Delarofs has an Aleut name meaning "hut."

Umiat, OO-mee-at (AA). Name of the airfield and oil exploration center on the Colville River is the plural form of *umiak,* the large, open walrus-skin boat used by the Eskimos.

Umnak Island, UHM-nak (SWA). According to Aleut legend, the name derives from *umnaqs,* meaning "fish line," as this island in the Fox group once boasted the Aleutian chain's only tree, which resembled the seaweed used by the natives to make fish lines.

Unalakleet, YOO-nuh-luh-kleet (WA). Recorded in about 1842 by Lt. L. A. Zagoskin, IRN, as the Eskimo village of "Ounalaklik," the community and adjacent river on the east coast of Norton Sound were given their present name spelling by the U.S. Board on Geographic Names in 1919. The name presumably derives from a term meaning "the southernmost one" in reference to the river south of the village.

Unalaska Island, UHN-uh-LAS-kuh (SWA). This large island in the Fox group bears a native name composed of two Aleut terms, *un* meaning "this" and *alashka* meaning "great land," to distinguish it from lesser islands in the Aleutian chain. The island's post office was once known as Ounalaska, but changed to the present spelling in 1898. Prior to the change, the village was romanticized in Thomas Campbell's poem, "Pleasures of Hope," as Onalaska and resulted in namesake towns in Wisconsin, Arkansas, Texas, and Washington. [*See* Alaska.]

Unga Island, UHNG-guh (SWA). Island bears the name of an Aleut village initially recorded as Qugnagok and adapted from a native word meaning "spout" in reference to some spout-shaped topographical feature.

Unimak Island, YOO-nuh-mak (SWA). Largest island (67 by 22 miles) in the Aleutian chain, this member of the Fox group bears an adaptation of the Aleut name Unimga, meaning "big one of them [the islands]."

Urey Point, YOOR-ee (SEA). Tip of land and rocks at the south end of Lisianski Strait in the Alexander Archipelago honor Capt.

Yurii Federovich Lisianskii, IRN, who explored the area in 1804–5 and helped Baranov regain Sitka from the Indians following the 1802 massacre at Mikhailovskii Redut. [*See* Lisianski Peninsula.]

Usibelli, YOOS-i-BEL-ee (IA). Named for Emil Usibelli, who established a coal mine in the locale in 1940.

Utukok River, oo-TOO-kahk (AA). An Eskimo name, meaning "ancient," applied by the natives to Icy Cape and subsequently extended by the Russians to the nearby river and to villages along its banks.

V

Valdez, val-DEEZ (SEA). The northernmost ice-free port in the Americas, the fledgling town of Copper City in 1898 adopted the name of the adjacent fiord extending inland from Prince William Sound. The waterway was named Puerto de Valdés in 1791 by Lt. Salvador Fidalgo to honor Spain's Minister of Marine Antonio Valdés y Basan. It was this celebrated Spanish naval officer who sponsored the survey of Alaska's coast by Alessandro Malaspina in 1791. Coincidentally, one of Malaspina's subordinate officers also bore the surname Valdés—Lt. Cayetano Valdés, who returned as commander of the *Mexicana* to explore north Pacific waters in 1792. [*See* Malaspina Glacier.]

Valley of Ten Thousand Smokes (SWA). Discovered in 1916 by a National Geographic Society expedition which gave the 17-by-4-mile valley a name descriptive of the smoke wisps and steam jets curling skyward. [*See* Katmai National Monument.]

Vancouver, Mount (SEA). The 15,700-foot-high peak astride the Alaska–Yukon Territory boundary in the Saint Elias Mountains was named in 1874 by William Healey Dall, USC&GS, to honor

Capt. George Vancouver, RN. During his 1790–95 voyage of exploration in the Pacific Ocean, Vancouver spent 8 months in Alaska waters and extensively explored—with the aid of his pilot, Master Joseph Whidbey—and personally named many of the islands and waterways in Southeastern Alaska. [*See* Admiralty Island; Lynn Canal.]

Vanderhoof (BC). Name honors Herbert Vanderhoof, a Chicago-based magazine publisher who promoted, under contract of the Canadian government and railroads, settlement of Americans in western Canada.

Venetie, VEN-uh-teye (IA). Village name and that of the Venetie Indian Reservation is a Kutchin Indian term of unknown definition.

Veniaminof Crater, ven-YAH-min-awf (SWA). The 8,225-foot-high volcanic mountain near the midpoint of the Alaska Peninsula was named in 1849 to honor Father Ioamn Veniaminov, the first bishop of Russian America. Born Ivan Popov-Anginski of humble parents in Siberia in 1797, he was renamed at a Greek Orthodox seminary in 1814 for a favored bishop and volunteered for missionary work in Alaska in 1823. After ten years among the Aleuts and five years at Sitka, he was recalled to St. Petersburg in 1839. His success among the natives, his study of their languages, and his scientific observations made him a celebrity with the church, aristocracy, and Tsar Nicholas I. He returned to Sitka in 1841 as Bishop Innokenti (Innocent). In 1850 he was recalled to Russia as an archbishop and in 1868 was named metropolitan of Moscow, the head of the Russian Church, by the emperor.

Verstovia, Mount, ver-STOH-vee-uh (SEA). Backdrop for the city of Sitka, this 3,300-foot peak was so named by Russian navigator Ivan Vasiliev (the first) in 1809 because it nearly reached the height of a *verst,* a Russian unit of measure equaling 3,500 feet.

W

Wainwright (AA). Community derives its name from that of the adjacent inlet by which Capt. Frederick W. Beechey, RN, honored astronomer Lt. John Wainwright of the expedition's H.M.S. *Blossom.*

Wales (AA). Village name derives from its location on Cape Prince of Wales at the tip of the Seward Peninsula, the most westerly point of the continent of North America. The cape was named in May 1778 by Capt. James Cook, RN, to honor his monarch's eldest son, Prince George Augustus Frederick, 1762–1830, who later ruled England as George IV. [*See* Prince of Wales Island.]

Walker Cove (SEA). This Behm Canal estuary was explored by Master Joseph Whidbey of the H.M.S. *Discovery* and named by Capt. George Vancouver, RN, for the expedition's surgeon, William Walker.

Walrus Islands (WA). Bearing a translation of the early Russian name of Ostrova Morzhovye, this group of small islands is but one of several features from the Aleutians to Point Barrow named for this mammoth-sized, tusked mammal which is allied to the seal family and indigenous only to the Arctic regions. Called "sea horse" by early English navigators, the walrus derives its name from the Old Norse language word *hrosshvalr,* meaning "horse whale."

Walter, Port (SEA). Three settlements—Big Port Walter, New Port Walter, and Little Port Walter—once graced the shores of the bay at the southern end of Baranof Islands. Despite the grandiose titles, the basic name, (Port) Walter, has no real significance, as it was arbitrarily assigned for charting purposes by the USC&GS in 1901.

Ward Cove (SEA). This suburb of Ketchikan was founded in 1883 by saltery operator W. W. Waud and the town was platted by and named for its first postmaster, Eugene Wacker, in 1920. The community was first called Wacker City, then Wacker, and in 1951 it was renamed Wards Cove, with the post office dropping the "s" in 1954. The community derived its name from its location on Ward Cove, which was named in the 1880s for one of the officers of the U.S.S. *Patterson,* a USCS survey ship.

Waring Mountains (AA). Named by Lt. George M. Stoney, USN, in 1886 presumably for a fellow naval officer.

Warren Island (SEA). Island off the west coast of Prince of Wales Island was discovered by Master Joseph Whidbey in 1793 and named by his commander, Capt. George Vancouver, RN, to honor Sir John Borlase Warren, British naval hero.

Wasilla, wah-SIL-luh (SCA). Matanuska Valley community was founded as an Alaska Railroad station around 1916 and named for the nearby creek which, in turn, was named for Wassilla, a Knik Indian chief.

Watson Lake (YT). The first community in the Yukon Territory reached by the northbound Alaska Highway traveler takes its name from the adjacent lake. It, in turn, was named for a Yorkshireman who stopped off in 1897 en route to the Klondike to prospect and trap in the Cassiar Mountains; he married an Indian woman and stayed on in the area until his death in 1938.

Waxell Ridge (SCA). The 26-mile-long ridge connecting Bering

and Steller glaciers in the Chugach Mountains honors Lt. Sven
Waxel, IRN, master of the *Saint Peter,* who assumed command
of the Russian exploration expedition upon the death of Vitus
Bering in 1741. [*See* Bering Sea.]

Wellesley Mountain (IA). Peak and lakes near the point where
the Alaska Highway crosses the U.S.-Canadian border were
named in the 1890s by the USGS for Wellesley College in Massachusetts. A glacier in the Chugach Mountains also honors the
same school and was named by the Harriman Alaska Expedition of 1899 in the course of their naming College Fiord and
several glaciers thereon for American universities.

Wells, Port (SCA). Name assigned by Capt. George Vancouver,
RN, in 1794 possibly to honor British geographer Edward Wells.

Whale Island (SCA). One of several geographic features whose
titles commemorate a vanishing species. Virtually depleted by
man in the nineteenth century—an estimated 100,000 killed in
Alaskan waters in the 1870s decade—the largest of mammals was
once common from the North Pacific to the Arctic Ocean. Its presence is reflected in such Alaska names as Whaleback Rock, Whale-
bone Cape, Whalehead Island, Whalers Creek, and Whaletail
Point. [*See* Beluga.]

Whidbey Passage (SEA). This waterway in Glacier Bay National Monument, a bay on the Kenai Peninsula, and a point
on Lynn Canal honor Master Joseph Whidbey, RN, senior
warrant officer of the Vancouver expedition that landed at the
mouth of Glacier Bay in 1794.

Whitehorse (YT). Capital of the Yukon Territory since 1953, the
city is the major population center in the territory and the northern terminus of the White Pass and Yukon Railroad from Skagway. Its name is taken from the Whitehorse Rapids in the Yukon
(Lewes) River, which were so named because the foam whipped
up by the churning waters resembled the mane of a white horse.
The local Indians, unacquainted with horses at the time the rapids

received their present title, called the spot Klil-has, meaning "very bad."

White Mountain (WA). Community takes its name from that of a nearby montain.

White Mountains (IA). Name descriptive of the mountains' white limestone composition.

White Pass (SEA). The name of the pass through the Coast Mountains utilized by the Skagway–Lake Bennett trail of '98 honors Sir Thomas White, Canadian minister of the interior. It was so named in 1887 following its survey by Skagway founder William Moore working under the direction of Dominion Surveyor William Ogilvie. Though White Pass was lower than Chilkoot Pass to the west, its route was longer and consequently less favored by most Yukon-bound gold seekers. It did, however, attract more pack trains than the easier Dalton Trail over Chilkat Pass, as evidenced by Dead Horse Gulch (Mile 19 from Skagway), which was named for the estimated 3,000 animals that died along the route. While the Chilkoot Pass initially was more frequently used—and was consequently more famous—than White Pass, it faded into disuse when the White Pass and Yukon Railroad was completed in 1900. [*See* Chilkoot Pass; Skagway.]

White River (YT). Named in 1850 by Hudson's Bay Company explorer-trader Robert Campbell for its white coloration caused by deposits of glacial silt and volcanic ash.

Whittier (SCA). This railroad port on the northeast coast of the Kenai Peninsula was established during World War II and adopted its name from the nearby glacier named by the USC&GS in 1915 to honor American poet John Greenleaf Whittier.

Wickersham Wall (IA). The west face of Mount McKinley (and a mountain, two domes, and a creek) honors James J. Wickersham, district judge and territorial delegate to Congress, who was the leader of an aborted attempt to climb the 20,320-foot South Peak of Mount McKinley in 1903. [*See* Fairbanks.]

Wien Mountain, WEEN (AA). Name honors pioneer Alaska aviator Noel Wien, one of four brothers involved in early-day aviation in Alaska—the land of the bush pilot. [*See* Merrill Pass; Orville, Mount; Wilbur, Mount.]

Wilbur, Mount (SEA). Peak in Glacier Bay National Monument was named by former Alaska governor and senator Ernest Gruening to honor Wilbur Wright who, assisted by his brother Orville, designed the first successful airplane. [*See* Orville, Mount.]

Wildwood (SCA). Former Wildwood AFS on the Kenai Peninsula bearing a descriptive coined name became in 1972 a school facility operated by the Alaska Federation of Natives.

Wilkes Range (SEA). Named in 1887 by a USN officer to honor Adm. Charles Wilkes who, as a lieutenant, commanded the United States Exploration Expedition of 1838–42 that circumnavigated the globe, explored the Antarctic islands, and charted much of the coastal and inland waters of Washington and Oregon.

Williwaw, Mount, WIL-ee-waw (SCA). So named by the Mountaineering Club of Alaska to commemorate six soldiers who died of exhaustion and exposure on its slopes when they were caught in the cold, gale-force winds, known as "williwaws," that rise suddenly in Alaska. The term derives from the Australian Aborigine name for cyclone.

Willow (SCA). A gold-mining camp in 1897 and subsequently a station on the Alaska Railroad, the settlement gets its name from the willow tree.

Wiseman (AA). Former mining town was named for prospector Peter Wiseman, who struck gold in the area of Nolan and Wiseman creeks. [*See* Coldfoot.]

Wolverine Peak (SCA). One of many geographic features in Alaska and the Yukon Territory with this faunal name. The largest member of the weasel family (*mustelidae*) is a physically strong scavenger with a voracious appetite and a notorious camp and trap raider that sprays a foul-smelling musk on whatever food he is unable to eat at the moment. Called "evil one" by the Eskimos, this northern North American predator has been labeled with a diminutive form of the word "wolf" because of its supposed fierce and blood-thirsty disposition. [*See* Cache Creek.]

Wonowon (BC). Town name was changed from Blueberry in 1954 to avoid conflict with a similarly named community in the province. The present name signifies the community's location at Milepost 101 on the Alaskan Highway.

Wood, Mount (YT). The peak in the Saint Elias range was named by an exploration expedition in the 1920s to honor Walter Wood, an official of the American Geographical Society and a member of the Arctic Institute of North America.

Woody Island (SEA). Name of the small island in Wrangell Narrows is a translation of Ostrov Lesnoi, the descriptive title assigned to the forested island by the Russians.

Wrangell, RANG-guhl (SEA). Established by the Russians as Fort Saint Dionysius in 1834 to block encroachment by the Hudson's Bay Company. In 1839 the Russian-American Company leased a portion of Southeastern Alaska to their British competitors, who changed the name to Fort Stikine. The USA established Fort Wrangell in 1868. During the Klondike Gold Rush era, the community was a key outfitting center for miners heading up the Stikine River. The names of the community and numerous other geographic features in the locale are derived from Ostrov Vrangelya, "Wrangell Island," by which the Russians were honoring Baron Ferdinand Petrovich von Wrangell, vice-admiral in the Imperial Russian Navy and governor of Russian America, 1830–35, when the original stockaded post was established. The 100-mile-long Wrangell Mountains north of the Saint Elias range and a 1,000- to 1,600-foot-high range on Attu Island in the Aleutians also are namesakes of the baron.

Wright, Mount (SEA). This peak in Glacier Bay National Monument, although near Mounts Orville and Wilbur, does not honor the flying Wright brothers. It is the namesake of Rev. Frederick Wright of Oberlin Theological Seminary, who as glacial geologist and scientific writer investigated the Glacier Bay area in 1886. A Mount Wright in the Alaska Range honors George M. Wright, who founded the Wildlife Division of the National Park Service in 1922.

Y

Yakobi Island, yuh-KOH-bee (SEA). Named presumably for Gen. Ivan Yakobi, chief of Russian colonial affairs, by Capt. Yurii Federovich Lisianskii, IRN, in 1804. [*See* Lisianski Peninsula.]

Yakutat, YAK-uh-tat (SEA). Town takes its name from the bay in the center of the Tongass National Forest. In the erroneous belief that Vitus Bering had landed there in 1741, the Russians called it Bering Bay; in 1786 French explorer Jean François de Galaup, comte de la Pérouse, named it Baie de Monti for one of his officers; the same year British trader Capt. Nathaniel Portlock dubbed it Admiralty Bay. In 1751 Capt. Alessandro Malaspina gave the head of the bay the Spanish title Puerto de Desengaño, which was loosely translated into English as Disenchantment Bay. To end the confusion, common usage reverted to the present Indian name stemming from the native words *yak,* meaning "ocean," and *tat,* meaning "salt-water estuary." The names given by La Pérouse and Malaspina linger on, however, as names of small bays on the shores of Yakutat Bay. [*See* Lituya Bay.]

Yanert (IA). Station on the Alaska Railroad derives its name from Yanert Fork. The river and the glacier in which it heads were named for Sgt. William Yanert, who explored the Susitna River area under command of Capt. Edwin Forbes Glenn, USA, in 1898. [*See* Glennallen.]

Yanovski, Mount, ya-NAHV-skee (SEA). Peak on Baranof Island honors Lt. Semeon Ivanovich Yanovskii, IRN, husband of Alexander Baranov's daughter Irina and the third governor of Russian America, 1818–20.

Yes Bay (SEA). Bay on the Cleveland Peninsula was initially called Yess Bay, an adaptation of the Tlingit Indian word *yas,* meaning "mussel."

Yukon Flats (IA). Descriptive name for the 200-mile-wide lowlands through which the Yukon River meanders at its northernmost point on the Arctic Circle. [*See* Yukon River.]

Yukon River. The name derives from the Athabascan Indian word *yukonna,* meaning "great river," according to records of Hudson's Bay Company traders who explored its upper reaches in the 1840s. The Eskimos living along the lower portion of the river and on its delta called it *kuikpak,* or "big river." The major river of the Alaska-Yukon region rises in a cluster of lakes in northern British Columbia approximately 15 miles from the Pacific Ocean and angles 2,300 miles through the middle of the Yukon Territory, turns west to meander nearly 1,500 miles across the center of interior Alaska to Norton Sound on the Bering Sea. The third longest river highway in North America, it is commercially navigable from its mouth to Whitehorse. Its major tributaries are the White, Lewes, Pelly, and Klondike rivers in the Yukon Territory, and the Porcupine, Tanana, Koyukuk, and Innoko rivers in Alaska. [*See* Fort Yukon.]

Yukon Territory. Named after its major river, the 205,346-square-mile territory is more than twice the size of Great Britain and larger than all of the New England states. Formed from the Northwest Territories of Canada in 1898, its first capital was Dawson, but the territorial seat was moved to Whitehorse in 1953. In addition to the Yukon and Klondike rivers, the major geographical feature is Mount Logan, 19,850 feet, the second highest peak in North America and the highest in Canada.

Yunaska Island, yoo-NAS-kuh (SWA). Located in the Islands of the Four Mountains, this island has an Aleut name of unknown meaning.

Z

Zarembo Island, zuh-REM-boh (SEA). Name honors Lt. Dionysius Federovich Zarembo, IRN, who captained survey ships in the area in the late 1830s.

Selected Bibliography

Adney, Tappan. *The Klondike Stampede.* New York: Harper & Brothers, 1900.

Aho, A. E. *Mining in Development of the Yukon.* Canada, 1970.

Akrigg, G. P. V. and Helen B. *1001 British Columbia Place Names.* Vancouver, B.C.: Discovery Press, 1969.

Armstrong, G. H. *The Origin and Meaning of Place Names in Canada.* Toronto: Macmillan, 1930.

Baker, Marcus. *Geographic Dictionary of Alaska.* United States Geological Survey, Department of the Interior, Bulletin 299. Washington, D.C.: U.S. Government Printing Office, 1906.

Balcom, Mary G. *Ghost Towns of Alaska.* Chicago: Adams Press, 1965.

Berton, Pierre. *The Klondike Fever.* New York: Alfred A. Knopf, 1958.

Colby, Merle (Works Progress Administration). *Guide to Alaska.* New York: Macmillan, 1943.

Dale, Paul W. *Seventy North to Fifty South: The Story of Captain Cook's Last Voyage.* Englewood Cliffs, N.J.: Prentice-Hall, 1969.

De Armond, Robert N. *Some Names around Juneau.* Sitka: Sitka Printing Co., 1957.

Geographic Board of Canada. *18th Report.* Ottawa: Department of Interior, 1924.

Gruening, Ernest. *The State of Alaska.* New York: Random House, 1954.

Henning, Bob. *The Milepost 1972.* Anchorage: Alaska Northwest Publishing Co., 1972.

Holmer, Nels M. "The Native Place Names of Arctic America." *Names*

15, no. 3 (September 1967): 26–40, and 17, no. 2 (June 1969): 138–48.

Hulley, Clarence C. *Alaska: Past and Present.* Portland, Ore.: Binfords & Mort, 1970.

Jacobsin, Lou. *Guide to Alaska and the Yukon.* Anchorage: Guide to Alaska, Inc., 1970.

Keating, Bern. *Alaska.* Washington, D.C.: National Geographic Society, 1969.

Keithahn, Edward L. *Alaska for the Curious.* Seattle, Wash.: Superior Publishing, 1966.

Krause, Aurel. *The Tlingit Indians: Results of a Trip to the Northwest Coast of America and the Bering Straits.* Translated by Erna Gunther. Seattle and London: University of Washington Press, 1970.

Marshall, James and Carrie. *Vancouver's Voyage.* Vancouver, B.C.: Mitchell Press, 1955.

Mathews, Richard. *The Yukon.* New York: Holt, Rinehart & Winston, 1968.

Middleton, Lynn. *Place Names of the Pacific Northwest Coast.* Seattle, Wash.: Superior Publishing, 1969.

Miller, Polly and Leon G. *The Lost Heritage of Alaska.* Cleveland, Ohio: World Publishing, 1967.

Mills, Stephen E. *Arctic Warbirds.* Seattle, Wash.: Superior Publishing, 1971.

Mills, Stephen E., and Phillips, James W. *Sourdough Sky: History of Bush Pilots in Alaska to 1940.* Seattle, Wash.: Superior Publishing, 1969.

Morgan, Murray. *One Man's Gold Rush.* Seattle and London: University of Washington Press, 1967.

Moziño, José Mariano. *Noticias de Nutka: An Account of Nootka Sound in 1792.* Translated by Iris Higbie Wilson. Seattle and London: University of Washington Press, 1970.

Mudge, Z. A. *Arctic Heroes.* New York: Phillips & Hunt, 1875.

Nanton, Paul. *Arctic Breakthrough: Franklin's Expeditions 1819–47.* Toronto: Clarke, Irwin, 1970.

Orth, Donald J. *Dictionary of Alaska Place Names.* Geological Survey Professional Paper 567, Department of the Interior. Washington, D.C.: U.S. Government Printing Office, 1971.

———. *North Slope Geographic Name Sources for Geologic Nomenclature.* Los Angeles, Calif.: Pacific Section, American Association of Petroleum Geologists, 1970.

Phillips, James W. *Washington State Place Names*. Seattle and London: University of Washington Press, 1971.

Ray, Dorothy Jean. "Eskimo Place-Names in Bering Strait and Vicinity." *Names* 19, no. 1 (March 1971): 1–33.

Rayburn, J. A. "Geographical Names of Amerindian Origin in Canada." *Names* 15, no. 3 (September 1967): 47–59, and 17, no. 2 (June 1969): 149–58.

Schwatka, Frederick. *Along Alaska's Great River*. New York: Cassell, 1885.

Sherwood, Morgan B., ed. *Alaska and Its History*. Seattle and London: University of Washington Press, 1967.

Stewart, George R. *American Place Names*. New York: Oxford University Press, 1970.

———. *Names on the Land*. Boston: Houghton Mifflin, 1967.

Swanton, John R. *Indian Tribes of North America*. Smithsonian Institution, Bureau of American Ethnology, Bulletin 145. Washington, D.C.: U.S. Government Printing Office, 1953.

Walbran, John T. *British Columbia Coast Names, 1592–1906: Their Origin and History*. Seattle: University of Washington Press, 1972.

Yukon Territory Community Survey. Whitehorse, Y.T.: Canadian Forces Northern, 1971.